Sailing, Yachts and Yarns

Tom Cunliffe

WILEY ✺ NAUTICAL

This edition first published 2011
© 2011 John Wiley & Sons, Ltd

Registered office
John Wiley & Sons Ltd, The Atrium, Southern Gate, Chichester, West Sussex, PO19 8SQ,
United Kingdom

Editorial office
John Wiley & Sons Ltd, The Atrium, Southern Gate, Chichester, West Sussex, PO19 8SQ,
United Kingdom

For details of our global editorial offices, for customer services and for information about how to apply
for permission to reuse the copyright material in this book please see our website at www.wiley.com

Library of Congress Cataloging-in-Publication Data

Cunliffe, Tom, 1947–
  Sailing, yachts and yarns / Tom Cunliffe.
      p. cm.
  Includes bibliographical references and index.
  ISBN 978-1-119-99283-7 (cloth)
  1. Sailing–Anecdotes.   2. Sailing–Miscellanea.   I. Title.
  GV811.C8725 2011
  797.1'24–dc22
                                    2010054181
A catalogue record for this book is available from the British Library.

WILEY ⊗ NAUTICAL

Wiley Nautical – sharing your passion.

At Wiley Nautical we're passionate about anything that happens in, on or around the water.

Wiley Nautical used to be called Fernhurst Books and was founded by a national and European
sailing champion. Our authors are the leading names in their fields with Olympic gold medals
around their necks and thousands of sea miles in their wake. Wiley Nautical is still run by people
with a love of sailing, motorboating, surfing, diving, kitesurfing, canal boating and all things aquatic.

Set in 12/14pt Garamond by Aptara Inc., New Delhi, India
Printed in Great Britain by TJ International Ltd, Padstow, Cornwall

CONTENTS

CONTENTS

FOREWORD

The first time I met Tom Cunliffe, he was carrying a brace of pheasants as he stepped out of a lift. Whether he'd shot them, run them over on his motorbike or they'd flown into his boat's rigging, I never discovered. The occasion of our encounter was my first *Yachting Monthly* Christmas contributors' party in 1989. The pheasants were a gift for *YM*'s then editor, Andrew Bray.

Two of the corner stones of *Yachting Monthly*'s success through the last 50 years have been promoting sound seamanship and sharing a good sense of humour. Two qualities which Tom has in abundance, along with his strongly held opinions. If you are invited to debate with Tom on the seaworthiness of some popular modern yacht designs, it may be best to decline. If you are an apologist for risk assessment, political correctness afloat and the Nanny State, prepare for the liveliest of disputes.

When a rogue wave gets ready to knock your boat down in mid-ocean, will you put your faith in a European kitemark from the Recreational Craft Directive or the wisdom of an old seadog? I know I'd rather ship aboard with Cunliffe any day than trust some slide-rule formula from a pen-pushing Eurocrat in Brussels.

The sea is the last great escape. And Tom is one of its staunchest defenders. You may not always agree with his outspoken views, but

FOREWORD

he can spin a good yarn with the best. Cunliffe is as irascible as he is indispensable and this collection of his columns makes an ideal bunkside companion from one of the great cruising commentators.

Paul Gelder
Editor, Yachting Monthly

INTRODUCTION

The short chapters that form this book are all columns that first appeared in *Yachting Monthly*. I am grateful to the publishers and the editor, my friend Paul Gelder, for making them available.

I had a false start as a writer back in the late 1970s when I strolled into the *YM* office on my return from an extended cruise to the Americas. I can't recall why that visit happened, other than my having some vague idea of easing my parlous finances by selling an article or two. Once inside, however, I realised that I was on hallowed ground. Over by the window sat the late Bill Beavis, whose 'Looking Around' column had been the witty and informative heart of the journal for many years. Bill said hello, then he led me into a back room where I met the great Des Sleightholme, editor and sailorman extraordinary. Des had taken over the reins of *YM* from Maurice Griffiths himself. Out on the shop floor, as it were, Andrew Bray and Geoff Pack were two aspiring young journalists. To my amazement, this august collection of talent took the trouble to encourage a tyro like me, and in due course a simple one-page article was bought in. I then went away sailing again and my pen remained in its box for many years. Finding myself in a mangrove swamp in Martinique with time on my hands during some unseasonable weather, I wrote a piece on star navigation and sent it to Geoff Pack. Geoff was a fellow old-school 'ocean walloper' and I hoped he might take the point. He did, and later reported that when he showed it to Andrew Bray – now editor – Andrew published it and told him to encourage me.

Looking back now over a quarter-century, the rest seems almost to have been preordained. I sailed my ancient pilot cutter home from the West Indies and made contact with the magazine. Andrew was beating the bushes in search of a Yachtmaster examiner to head up *YM*'s new seamanship initiative. The job was freelance, and it came my way. Column-writing followed naturally in the wake of this and of the many cruising features I submitted. The early writing years were taken up with semi-technical seamanship and navigation interspersed with extended breaks to go voyaging. It was only when Paul Gelder became editor that I was finally given the green light to say what I thought. He sent back a piece I'd written about some boat-handling knack or other with the comment that, 'there's more in you than this.' It was what I'd always wanted to hear.

Since that happy day, I've realised that being a columnist is a privilege. It's one of the few areas in journalism in which one may indulge one's personal thoughts. The magazine deliberately distances itself from the content, so the column gives it the opportunity to publish a viewpoint with which it may privately sympathise, but which it can, if need be, disclaim. For me, it's a lot of fun too. The sea is a colourful environment where characters abound. It offers a unique mirror to reflect on human nature, sometimes genuinely heroic, more often asking to be lampooned. I'm indebted to *Yachting Monthly* for allowing me my soapbox. Every month, I clamber onto it with relish and, like Bill Beavis before me, take another critical look around the horizon.

Tom Cunliffe, December 2010

HOLY COW!

Playing the blame game rarely proves a useful exercise, especially when a greater power has marked your card

Some thrive on uncertainty, others would turn the tide to avoid it if they could. Like it or not though, the only thing we can be really sure of at sea is that we never know what'll happen next. Last week, I dropped my biggest anchor on my foot. Was I unlucky, or was it my own stupid fault? There are arguments on both sides, but before examining what constitutes a genuine accident, it's worth sparing a thought for a crew of Japanese fishermen as reported in the *Australian Financial Review*.

These honest sons of the sea were cruising home mending their nets when a large cow fell from the sky, plunged through the deck before their astonished gaze, continued past the fish hold and out through the bottom. You might be thinking that the beast would have been better employed supplying milk to the thirsty, but the fishermen had other priorities because their boat was sinking rapidly. When they were

1

finally pulled from the water, nobody believed their story. Far from being returned to their loved ones, they were interrogated and slung in jail, presumably under suspicion of insurance fraud.

Weeks later, the truth was leaked by the Russian Air Ministry. Apparently the crew of a cargo plane had stolen a cow, herded her aboard, then taken off for home and a fresh beef dinner. The plan backfired somewhere over the Sea of Japan when the hitherto mild-mannered cudster awoke to the fact that her future looked short and far from pleasant. So violent were her berserk rampages that the aircraft's stability was compromised, leaving the airmen little alternative but to shove the beast out of the door. The chances of her making landfall on the boat below were so remote that not even Mr 'Jobsworth' the assessor could blame the fishermen. It just hadn't been their day.

We can contrast this misadventure with the affair of a young man in mid-ocean on a 21ft boat when his pressure-driven cooking stove ran low on alcohol half-way through supper. These units are considered by many as safer than propane, and lighting the rings follows a sequence. The fuel tank is pressurised with a hand pump with the supply to the burner turned off. The burner is now heated so that it will vapourise the fuel for combustion. This is done by igniting a small amount of raw alcohol tipped into an open pan under the base of the burner. With good timing, the pressurised fuel can be turned on just before the flames in the pre-heating pan die. If the burner is hot enough, the stove catches and roars into satisfying life. If it isn't, you either get the benefit of a jet of burning liquid fuel, or nothing at all. If you miss the right moment and the burner is hot enough, you're still in with a good chance of lighting it with a match.

Our gallant mariner's stew was nearly ready but, as the gravy warmed up, the fuel ran down until it became obvious he must refill it. Rather than go through the whole ritual, he opted to open the tank and top it up before the burner cooled off, then pump it up again while it would still work. He'd done it before, but this time his luck was out and an awkward wave spilled his fuel container onto the cooker. This flashed up all right, but not in the way he'd intended. His beard was burning merrily by the time he leapt over the side. So was the cabin as he struggled back on board, but his fire extinguishers were well sited to save his skin and his boat.

An unfortunate accident? I don't think so, do you? It is to this excellent adventurer's credit that he was able to complete a fine circumnavigation, but if it had ended there and then, he couldn't really claim to have been unlucky.

These contrasting catastrophes throw our more modest mishaps into perspective. We live in a culture of blame in which someone, somewhere must be held responsible for everything. If an out-of-control marina trolley pushed by a speed freak injures us as we sit minding our own business on a bollard, we probably have good reason to feel aggrieved. Accountability is less clear if we're hurt tripping over an unfair plank on a pontoon. Many would sue as a matter of course. Others might take the view that failing to look where we're going could just be our own fault.

Out at sea, it's no good complaining about who's to blame when things go wrong and urgent action is needed. The starting point for any subsequent investigation must be that we are responsible for our boats and actions, although accidents can happen from gear failures that the skipper couldn't be expected to anticipate. We might look to the manufacturer of a nearly-new winch whose pawls fail in normal use and break someone's arm with a flailing handle, but if a block that I didn't bother to inspect this year bursts, then whatever the consequences I have only two choices. Either I foolishly curse my luck or I blame myself like a gentleman.

Happily, however, there are still misfortunes for which we remain as guiltless as the fishermen sunk by the cow. When the sea breeze we hoped would kick in and blow us home turns unaccountably into a stiff headwind, it's either plain hard cheese or it's an Act of God. Submit all claims to The Almighty, c/o St Peter, Pearly Gates Yacht Club.

PASSING IT ON

The kindness of strangers is witnessed again and again at sea and along the waterfront

Long ago, I owned a traditional wooden boat that leaked. At sea it wasn't too bad because the worst of the cracks were between wind and water. So long as the planks were wet, they swelled nicely and kept her tight enough if you weren't over-fussy. I'd pumped her merrily across the Western Ocean early one summer then spent a couple of months working ashore in New England preparing for a late autumn run down to the Caribbean. The boat had sat still in baking heat and looked as though she'd dried out alarmingly. Ever the optimist, however, I foolishly listened to the dockside comforters who promised that the boards would soon take up at sea. Sadly, they did no such thing, and as the last of the putty was washed out from the seams behind the cooker I was able to enjoy a fine panorama of the passing Connecticut shore while brewing my tea. It was when a strand of seaweed curled into my docksiders that I came to my senses and dropped the sails. The leaking stopped as we straightened onto an even keel. I ran every pump I had and limped into a likely harbour to re-caulk the topsides.

Funds were in short supply, so I hung off a cheap dock upriver to employ the time-honoured technique of driving cotton into the wedge-shaped cracks before stopping it over with red lead putty. A week saw most of the job done, but half a dozen seams were so wide open after I'd cleaned them out that posting subscription copies of *Yachting Monthly* through them would have been a realistic possibility. The trusty cotton went straight through, so I tried oakum, the teased-out rope yarns soaked in Stockholm tar favoured by larger ships. That went the same way and I was seeking a viable alternative to suicide when an elderly man shambled up.

'Looks like you need a caulker, Son.'

'A new boat would be nice,' I muttered, eyeing my battered, dried-out planking.

The old boy peered intently into my seams.

'Plenty of life left in her yet,' he said. 'I've just the thing in my shed.'

Then he wandered off. Ten minutes later he was back, humping a coil of hemp warp and a clinking bag of caulking irons.

'This'll do the trick,' he said, unlaying the rope carefully. Without more ado he began stuffing the huge yarns into the waiting seams, and by evening the buildings echoed to the healthy ring of a caulking hammer whacking away at a sound hull.

'Good thing it was me found you and not my Uncle Albert,' observed the craftsman, stretching himself and stepping back. 'He taught me to caulk before the War when times were hard. You wouldn't have seen him wasting good rope. I've watched him do a job like this with welding rods. Leaked a bit to start with, but it all set up tight as a bottle once they rusted in.'

I shuddered and asked what I owed, but instead of a bill, he gave me some advice.

'No charge, boy. I can see you're tight for cash and I'm not busy. Just remember to pass it on one day. . . .'

I made it to the Caribbean and one windy afternoon I found myself anchored next to a very basic cruiser with a young couple on board whose ground tackle wasn't cutting the mustard. The toothpick and toilet chain thoughtfully supplied by their manufacturer would have held the boat for occasional fair-weather lunch stops in the Solent, but down here where the big winds boomed, they were a joke. The general ambience of the boat implied that they were stretched for funds and I was sorry for them, so in the end I surged an extra 10 fathoms of heavy chain for good luck and invited them to hang onto me for the time being. They hadn't been alongside long when a singlehander who looked as ancient as my caulker rowed across with a large anchor in his dinghy. It was just what the doctor ordered.

'Got a spare hook here,' he said to the young man. 'The wind won't ease for days and I'm away tomorrow. You can keep it.'

A 45lb CQRs didn't come cheap even back then, and the girl started to go through the motions of offering money with a hint of panic in her glance. The seagoing pensioner eyed up the situation.

'That pick's circumnavigated in my bilge and I never roused it out until now,' he said bluffly. 'So I don't need it, do I? I didn't expect to be richer when I woke this morning, and I'm no poorer now. I don't want cash. Just pass the favour on. . .'

Last week, I re-equipped with a new portable chart plotter which left me with a perfectly serviceable handheld GPS to spare. The nearest boat jumble beckoned, or a quick click into eBay, but I remembered that what goes around comes around, and knew exactly what to do.

UNCHARTED TERRITORY

Recent advances in navigation are just a drop in the ocean compared to the advances of the great cartographers

I remember as a small boy sitting at Christmas dinner with my father, a man blessed with a more than usually inquiring mind. For reasons now obscure, my elder sister and I were discussing the implications of the world being round. Thoughtfully, he helped himself to a spoonful of sage and onion, then he asked us if we could prove we lived on a sphere.

To say that we'd been told at school was not accepted. My Dad was not a navigator, but rigorous education had led him to a conclusion shared by everyone who really needs to know the truth. Whether this is how far off the rocks we are, or whether we can believe the newspaper, the common denominator is never to trust a single source of data without corroboration.

This placed his offspring on the intellectual spot. Nobody had then been in space to photograph Planet Earth as a shining disc, curved horizons were accounted for by perspective, he even contrived to discredit Phileas Fogg and other alleged circumnavigators. As the plates were cleared, however, he relented and showed how our point could be established by referring to a man named Eratosthenes.

Eratosthenes was a Greek philosopher, a chum of Archimedes. I don't suppose these two were a barrel of laughs on a night out back in 240 BC, but their mathematics shook the world. He had noted that the midsummer sun at noon shone straight down a well a few hundred miles up the Nile from Alexandria where he ran the library. Subsequently, he saw that on the same day of the year, it cast a measurable shadow outside his back door. From this, he calculated the globe's circumference based on the angular difference in the sun's height and the distance to the well. His principle was bang on and his numerical result wasn't far out.

I didn't give these issues any further thought until two days ago when I was turning the leaves of a late 15th century chart atlas drawn from empirical surveys originally collected by Ptolemy, another Greek, in around 150AD. His files had fallen into obscurity with the Roman Empire's collapse and didn't re-emerge until shortly before Columbus and Cabot put to sea, bound across the western horizon. The charts had rudimentary latitude and longitude. They also featured a form of conic projection, demonstrating beyond doubt that their author understood the spherical nature of the world he was depicting.

The rediscovery of Ptolemy's work burst on Europe like a thunderclap. Even if a little short of ARCS standards, here, at last, was proper cartography a sailor could use. Seafarers had, of course, employed linear distance as a measurable and repeatable factor for centuries. Without it there could be no Dead Reckoning, and without that, they were more or less lost. Things were looser on land. Here, the concept of the world shared by many is best understood by considering the Mappa Mundi, crafted in around 1290 AD. On my way to the Ptolemy Atlas in Hereford Cathedral library, I was shown this remarkable artefact, drawn on a single sheet of vellum. The Earth it portrays can only be described as chaotic. At first glance, it bears no resemblance to the real Europe, Africa and Asia it depicts, but closer examination indicates that if a Brit had it in mind to journey to Jerusalem, a rhumb line would correctly lead him across Greece. If he chose to keep his feet dry, he could leave Constantinople to starboard and go overland. Shortly after passing the Ottoman capital, he would however, travel by Noah's Ark, clearly marked along with a plethora of equally fanciful items.

The Mappa Mundi is really an encyclopaedia on a flat surface, designed to educate as much as to provide a passage-planning tool. This is an eye-opener on the mindset of the folk of that era. Only with the re-emerging Ptolemy maps and the hard-edged voyages of discovery that followed would man finally wake from the dreaming half-light of the Dark Ages into the sunshine of knowledge proven by experience.

The relevance of all this to us is surprisingly acute, living as we do in the immediate aftermath of a navigational upheaval. As I stood, fascinated by the stunning but ancient Mappa Mundi, it occurred to me that the revolution represented by the modern charts of Ptolemy to men like Cabot and Columbus leaves the recent eclipse of celestial navigation by GPS bobbing feebly in the broad wake of their caravels.

ON WATCH FOR EDDIES

Helping hands can be found in unexpected places down at the boatyard

Back in the harum-scarum years of the early 1970s, my wife and I subsisted on our boat in a Hamble River mud-berth. Our lives were in limbo between borrowing the cash to buy the ship and paying off the money-lenders so we could run away to sea. She made the more serious contribution to alleviating matters by organising the office of a well-known sailmaker; I limped along as a cruising instructor in between less reputable callings. Together with a community of ne'er-do-wells, we were moored stern-to on an ancient pier universally known as 'Debtors' Jetty' where Moody's Marina now stands (or did, until the family sold up). At its root was a gentlemen's convenience of the old school. Behind this stood a row of colourfully dilapidated medieval cottages, inhabited by a mix of longshoremen and one elderly deckhand who always wore brass buttons and a tie. It was said he had raced against the Kaiser.

On winter mornings at low water spring, my wife's journey to work began by clambering up a teetering gangway in the dark. She was then obliged to totter in high heels up the jetty with its inch-gapped boards to find whether her car, a yellow VW Beetle I'd bought in Southampton Auction for 50 quid, had been washed away by the midnight flood tide. Before she reached the gravelly foreshore that doubled as a parking lot, she had to run the gauntlet of a shadowy denizen of one of the cottages who made his living partly as a fisherman with a varnished teak oyster dredger, partly as the professional guardian of an equally well-finished yacht, and partly as a paid hand on a keelboat over at the Royal Yacht Squadron in Cowes. He was the last of a breed that had made the Southampton rivers famous for their seamen from the 1850s until WWII. Eddie was his name. Somehow, we always felt that he didn't think much of the likes of us.

Eddie started work at 0600 no matter how inky the pre-dawn winter blackness, and my wife could always tell if he was taking a break from mending his nets in the lee of the loo. He kept a fag bent on for what seemed 24 hours of every day and the glimmer of his gasper first thing in the morning gave him away every time. On one occasion shortly before Christmas, it was raining stair-rods as she set off on her dash up the dock. The wind had been howling all night and the boat had blown half-out of the hole she dug for herself in the ooze, so to add to the girl's usual catalogue of griefs, she had to negotiate the gangway at twenty degrees of heel. As for me, I was still turned in.

Her brolly whipped inside out as she stepped into the cockpit. By the time she came abeam of the gents she was already soaked to the skin. Eddie's Woodbine was smouldering like an intermittent glow-worm between her and the privy door as it creaked in the gale.

'Morning, Ma'am,' he said in his unique mock-friendly, mock-subservient tone. 'I see we've had the best of the day, then.'

To emphasise this ludicrous pronouncement, he performed his party piece, which was somehow to blow the ash off his cigarette end without removing either hand from his deep pockets. Now clear of the board-walk and on firm ground, my wife responded with more politeness than she felt, before fighting her way across to her motor which cruelly failed to start. Totally humiliated, she was about to step out into the storm when she was interrupted by a knock on the streaming window. It was Eddie.

'You stay put, now,' he said roughly. 'I'll turn out that young man of yours. We'll get you going.'

And so it was that just as daylight was crawling over the waving treetops I found myself bump-starting my wife's car with the last of the fisherman-yacht hands. I'd never been this close to him before and I noticed that he had a nasty wheeze, but he showed no signs of quitting after the second attempt failed. 'Keep way one, Nipper,' he gasped. 'No sense in giving up now...'

We kept on shoving, and the third time my bride dropped the clutch, the clapped-out flat four blattered into life. Her tail lights flickered on and she was gone into the tempest.

Last week, I saw the yacht that Eddie looked after all those years ago. She was far from the Hamble and someone had painted the varnished hull he once maintained so superbly, but there was no mistaking her. Crewed by strangers, she sailed by like a ghost from another life, but she brought two things to mind. A fine boat has many incarnations. Very likely she has good times and bad just as we do but, given her share of luck, she'll see us all out. The second thought was that it's a big mistake to prejudge people you meet around the waterfront until you're alongside them one stormy morning when friends are hard to find.

CUNLIFFE'S LAW OF DIMINISHING RETURNS

A summer cruise in company stresses the point that big isn't always better

Cunliffe's law of diminishing returns for time-limited cruising states that, 'A sailing boat's range increases as the square root of her waterline length. Her capacity to liberate her owner from his daily woes decreases by an equivalent factor.'

In plain English, this means a larger boat should get you there quicker, but that you may find yourself in the poor-house when you arrive.

In his wonderful book, *Dear Dolphin*, the late Frank Mulville remarks that when reduced circumstances obliged him to replace his lost 40-footer with a boat 10 feet shorter, fortune had done him 'no bad turn'. With Confucian insight, he also points out that, 'A man who buys a boat that is too big and expensive buys a treadmill.'

I've just come home from an afternoon at the Boat Show and once again I've been struck by how boats have grown. Thirty-eight feet isn't out of the ordinary for family cruisers these days, and few would consider venturing across the oceans with less than 40. Yet the truth of what Frank Mulville wrote has not changed. My own boat happens to be 40ft on deck and I'm a humble journalist who has to work for his money. Last summer, I cruised in company for a while with a pal in a 30ft Moody. We were both two-up and, apart from my yacht's commodious shower facilities, his boat did most of what mine could. On the short coasting trips we were making, my extra 12 feet of waterline didn't add up to much. Either he left half an hour earlier or he arrived a bit later, although on one occasion he nipped out with us and had made good so much distance by the time I had my heavy sails drawing that I spent the rest of the afternoon catching him up in light airs. He would probably have found really foul weather more challenging than me, but we chose decent conditions so when I began weighing up my concrete advantages I didn't find many. One afternoon, I met him tottering out of the harbourmaster's office as I was tip-toeing in. His hand was clapped to his brow.

'You OK, Mate?'

'I just got banged for 20 Euros!'

When I came across him later in the Bar du Port, my own wallet was 30 Euros the lighter and he was laughing all the way to the hole in the wall. That started us talking and I soon realised why he was eating in better restaurants than me. A new mainsail for his boat was less than half of one for mine. His antifouling bill seemed tiny, his annual insurance premium could have been covered by a decent case of claret, while mine would have bought my young daughter a viable used car. The list went on and soon I was remembering some hard facts about good times and smaller yachts.

Years ago, I lived and cruised happily in a wooden classic with 5ft 8in headroom under the main skylight and five feet everywhere else. I am 6ft 6in tall. Back in 1980, the National Sailing Centre used to run Competent Crew courses on Contessa 32s with six people on board for a week. I won't say life was luxury, but we had more fun than is considered legal nowadays. Lin and Larry Pardey sailed round the world and back in a beautifully fitted-out 25-footer. When they changed up to 30 feet they must have wondered what to do with all the space.

On the other side of the coin, a typical summer cruise for me involves passages of several days' duration. Six hundred miles up to Norway, perhaps, or a Biscay crossing. As soon as my boat eases her sheets with a fair wind, she hardly knows how to do less than six knots. Although a smaller yacht might arrive only a day or so later, the emotional benefits of literally striding the seas are considerable. A bit of extra tonnage is reassuring if you're caught out by an unseasonable gale, and it eases the pain if the years have downgraded the flexibility of your joints. Furthermore, if all else about two boats is equal, the larger will be the better load carrier – my tanks hold 220 gallons of water, for example. One way and another, if a yacht's going to be remote from civilisation for long periods, some owners might feel that the massively increased costs are worth bearing. The real question is, how many 40-footers actually fulfil their potential?

Most who go to sea rate 'freedom' as a priority, yet perfect freedom remains an illusion until all financial cares are lifted. This can only be achieved in two ways. Either the sailor has adequate resources in place to live and cruise anywhere, without compromise, for as long as he chooses, or his needs are small and he works his way along within a mind-set of self-sufficiency. The majority fall somewhere between the two. We may be having a fine time of it, but our ability to go when and where we please is limited by our circumstances.

In light of this, a simplified Cunliffe's law should find few dissenters next spring when the mooring bills drop on the doormat like depth charges: 'Happiness increases with deliverance from care and is indirectly proportional to waterline length.'

TOGETHER IN THE END

A special ceremony off the coast of France flags
up the way the sea unites us all

M ost islanders' default assumption is that their own speck of
land is the centre of life. Look at us Brits. Intellectually, we
know it's not true but, deep in our genes, a rogue strand still
pushes this archaic view. To a Franco-Roman standing on Cap Gris Nez,
Britons living behind the white cliffs on the horizon were as foreign as
Men in the Moon. From some perspectives, little has changed, but every
so often my English streak is jolted into recognising that we are closer
to other people than we might think. Take last summer for instance.

My wife and I were chilling out, running the tides and cruising some
of our favourite North Brittany haunts. As usual, we'd stopped over
in St-Quay Portrieux, not for its delights as a venue, but because it is
one of the few all-tide harbours in the Bays of St Malo and St Brieuc.
Make do with a night in this highly professional port and you can
plan the tides for a drying haven of your choice. We left the marina
at dawn, ghosted across the big bight of reef-strewn sea and arrived
off Dahouët just before Saturday lunch. Once inside the sheltering

breakwaters of natural rock only revealed at low water, my gaff cutter received a surprising greeting from an ecstatic harbourmaster.

'You are here for the festival, M'sieur?'

I'd never heard of any festival but, always one for a party, I asked for further details. It proved to be the twentieth anniversary of the opening of the tiny, sill-locked marina and also of the launching of the town lugger. The event ran for two days and included the usual fun, free booze, fellowship and fireworks. All we had to do was sit tight in the plum berth to which we were ushered and a good time was, we were assured, guaranteed.

'And of course, for you there is no charge.'

'You mean, nothing to pay?' This was not the sort of official I was used to meeting on my own side of the Channel, where all too many grab their calculators to see how much extra they can screw out of me for the bowsprit.

'To have so beautiful a boat in our port is a privilege.' He replied simply.

This promising start was well fulfilled. That night, we ate sardines on the quay with the harbourmaster and his wife, the fishermen and the Parisians who were making the most of the local colour. The squeeze-boxes wheezed, the dancers twirled, and one bottle led to another, as they do, but by sun-up I was back in basic working order. As I went on deck to tuck into my 'crescent' and drink my coffee, I met our neighbour, a powerfully built local with a large sailing yacht. He had brought a gigantic bouquet which he set down carefully on his coachroof.

'This morning,' he answered my unspoken question, 'we go out and lay flowers on the sea. It is for those who have perished in deep water. This year is special for me. I own ten trawlers. One was lost last winter. With eight men.'

Having no wheels and being far from the nearest florist, we two Brits strolled out into the fields after breakfast and picked a bunch of wild flowers which we lashed up with tarred marline. When the boats put to sea at the top of the tide, we followed them under short canvas. With jib and main we had perfect control, and by keeping our staysail and topsail in their bags we didn't take off in our usual scalded cat imitation. As we passed through the tight, cliff-lined entrance, a white-clad priest was leading a long procession up to the shrine of Notre Dame de la Garde which overlooks the narrows. They were carrying the effigy of Our Lady shoulder-high and intoning a repeated prayer.

Out at sea, we cruised to and fro for a while wondering what to do, until we noticed a modern trawler hove to a cable to seaward of the cliff-top shrine. Boats were slowly passing her port side and we saw one toss a posy onto the sea. We tacked over and headed into the crowd. For a moment I wondered if we would find a way through the close-packed fishing boats, but as our towering rig approached, they melted aside like snow, allowing us free passage to the trawler. Sailing by 15 feet from her bulwarks and casting our flowers in memory of our own drowned as well as theirs, we saw the Curé, fully robed and standing on her fish hatch, blessing the boats and blessing us too. A splash of holy water flickered across the blue sea and then we were hardening up, leaning on the wind to clear the throng.

As we cruised back to our berth, I reflected that at sea, there are no English dead and Breton dead. Those who perish in the ocean are an international community. Islander or Continental, in the final roll call, we are all one.

JONAH AND THE WAVE

A clumsy crewman teaches a useful lesson in storm survival

D o you ever spare a thought for poor old Jonah, tossed overboard by his fellow mariners as being responsible for a nasty spate of weather? The biblical account advises that Jonah's famous storm arose because he had side-stepped some onerous commission laid on him by the Almighty. It's not for us to question The Word, but speaking for myself I've known a few Jonahs and most of them weren't on the run from divine retribution. They were just accident-prone guys who seemed to spread their own ill luck over the ship at large. Consider Oddjob for example, a shipmate of mine who got his name from sailing in a hat like a hard-brimmed bowler.

Oddjob and I were delivering a 50ft motor fishing vessel to the French Riviera. My usual team couldn't make it and Oddjob turned up from a crewing agency with his mate, Jack. The first night out, one of the two engines over-heated and blew up during Oddjob's watch after he mistook the warning whistle for the kettle boiling. Hard luck, you might say, and at the time I did. We limped into Guernsey, had the diesel rebuilt, then pressed on.

Oddjob delivered his next catastrophe in Lisbon. After topping off his requirements in a dockside bar towards midnight, he stepped over the sea defence wall to pump ship, slipped on the slimy boulders and slithered into the dark water.

'That's it lads!' he called, flapping his arms feebly as a ripping ebb carried him seawards along the stonework. There seemed little to be gained from jumping in after him, so Jack legged it back to the ship for a heaving line while he clung precariously to a strand of seaweed. We hauled him out, rubbed him down and he swore to lay off the booze in future. But they all say that, don't they?

I'd almost forgotten Oddjob's tendencies when we ran into a full-blown Mistral on the last lap of the trip. We were taking big seas on the beam and it should have been no surprise when an awkward breaker arrived half-way through Oddjob's afternoon watch. It threw us down unceremoniously into the trough, leaving Jack and I buried beneath a pile of debris below under the lee deckhead.

'I wonder what happened to Oddjob,' mused Jack as the ship righted herself and we scrabbled back to the cabin sole. The wheelhouse proved empty of bodies and Oddjob's yellow oilskins had gone from their peg. It appeared he'd left us. Hoping he'd wandered on deck for a smoke, we pushed open the door, but there was no sign of him out in the storm. Jack throttled back while I peered frantically across the grey waste of the ocean for any trace of our shipmate. I was asking myself whether perhaps the gale would now mysteriously subside, when I heard a feeble voice calling my name. It was his all right, but it seemed to come from the heavens. For a second I feared he was already an angel, until I glanced up and saw his round hat silhouetted against the sky above the wheelhouse.

'I'm up here, boys. . .'

Oddjob had been washed clean overboard as the boat was knocked down. He'd spent a few seconds thrashing around considering his immortal soul until, like Jonah before him, the ocean spat him out. With the boat still on her side, and lacking the convenience of a passing whale, a second sea had tossed him against the lid of the house. He'd embraced the radar scanner for a free ride while she righted, and had remained there dazed while we presumed him dead and gone.

Jack set the autopilot to head slowly into the waves while we dried out the swimmer for the second time. When we returned to the helm we were impressed by the change in motion. Gone were the violent lurches of a small craft in a dangerous beam sea. Instead, she remained upright, rolling gently and nodding as she soared up the steep faces of the swells, breasted the peaks and nudged down their windward sides. We hoisted a reefed mizzen, sheeted it board flat to steady her and steered just far enough off the wind to fill it most of the time. We made virtually no headway but maintained enough steerage to keep her bow up to the crests. We steered manually to dodge any breakers until conditions took a turn for the better.

A week later I was safe in St Tropez with the hands paid off. I've often speculated about what became of Oddjob, but there was no doubt that once he stepped ashore, the drama factor tangibly diminished.

The technique Jack and I stumbled across is well known by fishermen as 'dodging'. Until recently it has not been considered a yacht survival option, but things have changed. In heavy airs and big seas a roller reefing genoa is useless. The nature of many modern yachts means that they must never be allowed to lie beam-on to seas steep enough to break yet, unlike their predecessors, they cannot shoulder them by heaving to. Running before the storm is fine, but alert crew and searoom are a prerequisite. Neither may be available. The para-anchor is a sound proposition, but many boats don't carry one. What most of today's cruisers do have is a powerful, reliable engine. Using this at moderate revs backed up by a rag of flattened mainsail to head up into an ugly sea has become a practical survival option. Dodging makes sense for the ordinary cruiser caught without specialised gear by a summer gale.

It doesn't take a Jonah to cause a knock-down. The wrong wave will manage that nicely if we give it a chance, but using the engine sensibly can save us asking for a volunteer we can throw to the fishes.

LESSONS LEARNT FROM
A PUFFIN

Many a modest adventurer of the past would
have been stymied by today's sea of red tape

A large bonus that comes with writing about yachting is that a
stream of interesting material lands on my desk. Today's arrivals
provided a stark glimpse of how attitudes to sailing are changing.
Nobody can halt the march of time, but when I read this morning's
offerings I couldn't help reflecting on the stresses of modern life.

The first item was a tiny cameo of a book which my wife, who
collects sailing literature by women, had ordered. I dipped in, and
was captivated. *Puffin's Log* (ISBN 978-0-9561469-0-8) is about family holidays on a diminutive wooden yacht in the early 1950s. The
work is illustrated with charming sketches and watercolours, plus a few
monochrome photographs. The text is deliciously uncomplicated. The
21ft yacht has the tightest of headroom and a minute petrol engine
whose consumption would be measured in pints, so little was it used.
There is only one pair of bunks, but a mattress tossed up into the focsle

affords modest comfort at bed-time to the two small girls. The son, somewhat older, dosses down on spare sails between his parents.

Puffin lives on a mooring half a mile out in Poole Harbour, probably at the cost of a few shillings a year. The writer, Jocelyn Greenway, does comment that their holidays are very economical. They row out, come wind or weather, in a clinker-built dinghy which they then tow to wherever they are going. The children are encouraged to use this to develop their seamanship skills, which, of course, in the absence of an outboard engine, they do. When it rains in harbour, things are a bit tight, but somehow they manage. They cruise to the Solent and all the usual South Coast destinations, but they also spend time in the Seine Bay and twice make it to Holland and the Ijsselmeer. This is good going by any standards in such a craft which, you'll note, doesn't even have a self-draining cockpit, much less VHF radio, liferaft and all the other paraphernalia without which many of us wouldn't leave harbour.

Irresponsible? You could say that, but I won't. Robert Greenway had just come through WWII, fighting in India and Burma. He was a qualified architect and a university lecturer. A man of experience few of us can equal, and no fool. The love and care for one another which shines through his wife's accounts are simply a joy, and we can be grateful to their daughter Cathy for having the logs bound and published.

My breakfast reading was rounded off by a session with the RYA Magazine. I contribute to this from time to time, so I'm certainly not going to knock it. In fact, the RYA do well in monitoring what the authorities have dreamed up next to make our lives a misery, and at least trying to keep the worst excesses in check. Here, instead of reading about sensible people making up their own minds as to what was safe and what wasn't, I found reports of convoluted regulations suggesting the eminently sensible LED navigation lights a friend just fitted to his yacht may not be acceptable under the regulations. For your information, the rules in question are brought to our attention by 'MGN393'. 'MGN', by the way, is 'Marine Guidance Notice' to you!

Next, I discovered that Health Care charges are no longer covered in the Channel Islands (I wonder if Mr and Mrs Greenway would have cared), and that when purchasing red diesel in the UK, I must request the retailer to mark the invoice or receipt as 'duty paid', logging the date and engine hours to reinforce the record. I also discovered that if I put the stuff in a can, I'll be in dire trouble.

We need to know these things, of course, because those who would rule us keep piling on the agony, but the contrast with 50 years ago as evidenced by *Puffin's Log* is stark. You can't argue with the fact that, if we comply with every regulation, and load our boats up with the recommended life-saving kit and backup navigation systems, we'll probably be less likely to come unstuck than the Greenway family. The message of my morning reading, however, has been that to accept this without looking further into the question is to miss the point of why we go sailing.

Today's standards tend to concentrate on what we might call 'secondary safety'. This is about buying things that may give us another chance when the boat has failed us or we have failed ourselves. Primary safety, on the other hand, is about having a well-found yacht that is properly seaworthy in shape and displacement, then operating her in a seamanlike manner. The European Small Craft Directive wouldn't give *Puffin* many points, yet the Greenways enjoyed years of adventurous cruising and never came to grief. Knowing what I now do about the character of the people, I wouldn't put this down to good fortune. I conclude that they kept a weather eye out for trouble and steered well clear of it. By avoiding obsession with gear, or paying huge money for a yacht far bigger than they really needed then relying on others for their ultimate survival, their stress levels stayed at rock bottom. You've only to read Jocelyn's account and see the art that Robert found time to produce to feel their inner peace.

As I remarked at the outset, we can't turn back the clock, but we'd be crazy not to learn a few lessons from the Greenways.

IN THE DRINK

Three overboard incidents emphasise the usefulness of modern recovery equipment

B ack in the late 1960s I ran a small sailing school near Marseilles.
We had a fleet of dinghies and a seaworthy open lugger which I
used as a safety boat. When the Mistral came rattling down the
nearby Rhone valley the dinghies were grounded, but I kept the show
on the road with somewhat hairy picnic trips in the lugger. The policy
was to hug the lee of the land, but on one occasion I had a lively crowd
who fancied a walk on the wild side. So out to sea we went, reefed so
deep you could reach up and touch the yard.

I was aft at the tiller to windward and we were all eating baguettes
when there was a bit of a kerfuffle up forward behind the foot of the sail.
I thought nothing of it until I happened to glance astern to see one of
our likely lads bobbing in the wake. This was in the days before the RYA
method and nobody had taught me anything about Man Overboard
drill, but I was a decent enough sailor. A dipping lugger isn't the easiest
of craft to manoeuvre, but one way and another we wrestled her around.
With some muscular assistance from willing young hands at the heavy

oars, she came alongside our victim in the roaring gale like a swan on a lake and we were able to heave him bodily inboard. We all had a good laugh, he went back to his baguette and I got going again. As easy as that. It was only when I became a 'proper' sailing instructor some years later that my blood began to run cold thinking about all the things that could have gone wrong.

My second 'MOB' came at the end of a long two-handed ocean passage in a boat without an engine. My wife and I were preparing to anchor off a palm-fringed beach in a stiff breeze and I was swigging up the topping lift when my day took a turn for the worse. The rope was an ancient length of manila. Even back then you didn't see much of this venerable material, and I'd been wondering about its condition for a while. The strands seemed to be growing longer and it was taking on an ugly grey sort of colour instead of the beautiful buff so beloved of Dutch old masters. To cut to the chase, the boom was heavy and I was throwing my whole weight outboard when the topping lift parted. There was only one way for me to go, and I went. My wife tells me that I executed a back flip with half-turn and pike before I smacked into the drink with a splash like a breaching whale.

This, of course, left the lady solo-sailing a gaff cutter with no engine, feeling obliged to pick me up into the bargain. When it comes to certification, she still doesn't have a Competent Crew ticket, and I had time to reflect on how little training we'd done as she cruised round for her first pass. The sight of a 32-foot boat ripping straight at you when you're a bit shocked is not conducive to calm and tranquillity, but she steered away at the last minute and surged past. By the time she returned, I'd thanked my maker in every way I knew for not allowing that line to let go out at sea the night before as I reefed in the moonless tradewind. I'd have been dead for sure. As it was, my bride spilled wind like a professional on her second time around, lost way a boat's length to windward and tossed me the tail of a spare halyard. I swarmed aboard up the bobstay and that was that.

A third incident that ended with an unscheduled swim came while I was a charter skipper. One of the guests was a remarkable character who'd studied at Eton and Oxford, sparred with a professional heavy-weight boxer who is still a household name, and played front row forward for Castleford. At the time he sailed with me, he was doing very well in business. The yacht was anchored off and the charterers had decided to go ashore for a serious dinner. The gentleman was lining up for the dinghy, wearing a full tux; a glass of brandy in one hand and a Churchill cigar in his mouth. As he stepped down into the RIB, he turned to crack a joke to one of the girls. The RIB was only attached by a painter and it skidded away smartly, leaving a three-foot gap into which he tumbled, bum-first. It was now that he showed his class. He held the five-star Hennessy high over his head and somehow contrived to keep the cigar burning without ever touching it. He was a mountain of a man, and helping him back on board would have been a challenge had he not been extremely fit. Within minutes, he was on parade again with the same smoke clenched securely between his teeth. It made you proud to be British.

I mention these events because it's early in the season, and every year I have to remind myself how vulnerable I really am. Today, firms like Raymarine are producing GPS man overboard alarms that not only tell you when someone's gone, they also guide you unerringly back to any casualties because they're carrying their own GPS transmitters. It wouldn't have done much for my charterer, but I'm still sailing with just my wife. The thought of punting around the ocean on a dark night searching for one another doesn't bear thinking about. I reckon I'm off down the chandler's right now, but I'll still be double-checking the safety harnesses.

HERE'S HOPING

The globe may seem to be shrinking, but that's no reason to forget the pleasure that can be found between destination and arrival

I've an old tin plate that sits on the shelf in my study. Long ago it served on board as a vehicle to transfer the five-day stew from pan to spoon, but since I re-equipped the crockery locker with more attractive wooden ones it's been redundant. A shame in a way, because around its faded rim runs a legend that has helped me through many a nasty night at sea. Although no longer half-obscured by gravy, its fairy-clean, battered enamel still proclaims that, 'To travel in hope is a better thing than to arrive.'

Oddly enough, this sailor's mantra came to mind recently when looking around for a better deal than I'm currently getting from my web server. 'Try India,' said my neighbour, a man who knows about such things. 'India,' I thought, and my traveller's soul stirred. 'How about this: we fly to Calcutta, hire a couple of motorbikes and ride up the Great Trunk Road under the Himalaya until we discover a software guru. . . . ?'

'Or we could just surf the internet,' was the sensible response, 'then nip down the High Street for a quick Vindaloo in the Taj Mahal.'

I couldn't argue with his logic, but this was hardly the spirit that built the Empire. It wasn't just nailing the computer whiz that was turning me on, it was the journey for its own sake.

You'll have noticed that boats are getting bigger. Time was when a family was content with a 30-footer. Some managed well with far less; so did many an ocean walloper. The longer waterlines and reliable engines of today have encouraged ever-faster passage times until many of us find we're thinking of the end almost before we've set off. I do it myself. A generation ago, the trip up to Holland from the Solent could well have taken three or four days. Today, I can blast off with a tank-full of diesel, use it where necessary to keep my average boat speed up to six knots, and be in Flushing 36 hours after leaving Pompey. This encourages a sort of 'sprint mentality'. If we aren't careful, it turns passage-making into something we need to have done with in order to place our order in the Bar van Hooligan, or buy a bunch of daffs.

Contrast this with the comments of the sexton I once met in an ancient wooden church on one of the remoter Åland Islands. I'd had a time of it getting there, what with uncharted rocks, a Baltic northerly and the rest, and I'd popped in late in the evening for a bit of peace. Beside the path to the porch a half-dug grave gaped at me, and a shovel was propped beside the studded door. In the pitch-pine silence inside, a votive ship hung from the rafters, illuminated by the low sun streaming through a slit window. She was a four-masted barque of the type used by the local Eriksson line on the Australia run as late as 1939.

'What do you think she's doing there?'

I'd imagined myself alone, so the rough voice caught me flat aback. Turning, I saw an elderly man in working clothes who had clearly just refreshed himself from his hip-flask. He was the gravedigger.

I replied that perhaps the big model was donated in thanks for a delivery from danger, or maybe as an oblation to protect local seamen.

'That's what they're for down in Spain,' continued the man in perfect English, obviously a far-travelled sailor himself. 'Here, they remind us that life's a voyage and we can't get off the ship. A trip in an aeroplane isn't even an excursion. It's just a rush from one place to another. On a sailing ship, a passage can easily last four months. That's part of your time on Earth. You can't always love your shipmates, but you find ways of living with them.'

His message was clear. It's exciting to arrive, but the long watch between departure and landfall is the thing.

Here's another aspect to it. We're designed for a planet that has a certain size in relation to us. It's fashionable to talk about the shrinking Earth, but in our own primeval terms, the globe remains unimaginably huge. Until recently, distance was understood in terms of how far somewhere was to walk, or maybe ride a horse. Modern transport has hacked this perspective to pieces. A good thing too, in many ways, but its broad wake carries a distorted view of our own slot in the world. It's salutary to sail to America and to realise that rather than being a quick seven hours on the red-eye flight, the place is a serious distance off indeed. Days run into weeks, the weather sends what it will and we must make the best of it because, as the sexton said, there's no getting off. The trip measures a real percentage of our days. On a smaller scale, the same thing applies when cruising locally, so I for one am going to slow down this year. Perhaps if I burn my wooden plate and reinstate the old faithful it'll remind me to rejoice in the moment. The reality of arrival sometimes disappoints. While it lasts, the journey of hope never does.

GLAD TO BE TRAD

Regular routines can take on great significance for a sailor

Tradition. What's it worth? Like all the best questions, this one doesn't have a simple answer. Easter isn't far away and the wine bins at the homestead are getting low. If the weather is halfway decent, the likelihood is that on Good Friday I'll be in mid-Channel with my family, bound out for an early-season raid on the 'Caves' of Northern France. We've been making this annual pilgrimage since before my grown-up daughter was born and you'd think we'd all be fed up with it by now, but we aren't. Judging by the number of sails we'll be watching going our way, neither are hundreds of other South-coast sailors anxious to remind themselves of the joys and horrors of our calling. Sometimes, it seems like a lot of trouble and when the forecast is for rain we're tempted to forget it, but we make an extra effort year after year because we don't want to break with tradition.

I've no idea what goes on aboard the other yachts, but in our galley another institution will be in full swing. This one has nothing to do with the sea. It goes back to my childhood, where I learned it from my grandmother in a terrace near the wharves in Sunderland, who had it from her own forebears. As the boat heaves and lurches her way south, we will be busily engaged stripping the outer skins from a pound or two of onions. We'll wrap these around a dozen fresh eggs, tying them gingerly in place with sail twine. Once prepared, the eggs will be boiled hard and left in the pan to cool, where they'll take on the most fantastic tie-dyed brown and orange patterns. They are now 'Pace Eggs', the original Easter Egg that predates today's chocolate confection by centuries. On Easter morning, to the consternation of the French, we roll these competitively along our side decks. Just as it was back in Dock Street, the one that travels furthest 'gets the coconut'. The prize is immaterial. Generally there isn't one, except for the satisfaction of a victory won squarely, on a tipsy playing field strewn with chain plates, cleats and fairleads.

The word 'Pace' has no English root that I can find. Other countries, of course, don't call the spring equinoctial festival 'Easter'. It's 'Pâcques,' in France, 'Pascua' in Spain and 'Pasqua' in Italy, so although our language lost its way down the long road since the Romans left, somewhere in the fastnesses far to the north of Watford, the torch of civilisation still flickers. As for the rolling process, perhaps it refers to that greater question, 'Who rolled the stone?' that sealed Christ's tomb. I don't expect ever to know. It's enough that I trundled my Pace Egg with Grandma and that my offspring follow on. It's a family tradition that connects the smallest living members of our tribe with unknown ancestors who would otherwise be lost to us forever.

Once, I made an extended cruise in the company of a hero. He never missed his watch, never lost his temper and, it must be said lest he be thought a saint, never failed to point out the error of my ways. He didn't hang back when there was hard work to be done; he was tough, literary, a philosopher. This remarkable individual didn't even eat much, yet none of these exemplary characteristics qualified him for the accolade of Superman. This was awarded for the pride he took in attending to the ship's flag etiquette. In another life he had been a professional hand aboard one of the great yachts of the previous generation, and he would no more sleep through 0800 than miss the chance for a nip of my best rum when it was offered. At 0759 he'd be up on deck, rain or shine, fresh-faced or suffering the sort of hangover that would stun a racehorse, unrolling the 2-yard ensign. Cold on the stroke of eight, checked by the ship's navigation chronometer, up went the colours, followed by the club burgee. In the tropical evenings, as the sun bit the horizon bound on its nightly passage for Panama and points west, he took them in again and stowed them with proper reverence.

That's another tradition that binds us to a past we can be justly proud of. To let it slip breaks a link in the chain that defines who we are.

FIGHT FOR THE WIGHT

Plans to build a marina in an Isle of Wight harbour threaten an endangered species*

For the big motor yacht that's only really comfortable hooked up to the National Grid, marinas have a lot going for them. Even sailing-yacht owners have been known to subscribe to a permanent berth, but marinas do have their drawbacks. If you have a swinging mooring on the Clyde, you'll laugh loud and long to learn that the poor sap cruising the South Coast in a 35-footer can rack up a bill of two hundred quid in a week without really trying. Harbour companies will point out that for a crew of five this represents little more than the cost of a round of drinks or two. The flaw is that most of us don't sail with the rugby club on board. Often it's just two plus, maybe, the kids. If we weren't planning on going to the pub, that's a big hole in the holiday money.

*Power to the People! As of March 2011, a compromise of sorts is in uneasy existence. The wall-to-wall marina plans are not quite on hold, but seem to have been diluted at least to some extent. All is not lost.

Far more important than the cash are the madding crowds. Even a busy anchorage doesn't cram us together in anywhere near the same way. Wildlife isn't generally thrilled about the march of the pontoon monster across its habitat either, in spite of all the eco-studies and consultations. It's one thing to slip on a duck-turd, significantly deposited on your pontoon by a feathered benefactor; it's another altogether to witness the dawn flight of mallard as they rustle into the sky over the windswept marsh, bound in freedom for who knows where. Perhaps the most insidious side-effect of all, however, is the wretched sameness of marinas. Take the small town of Yarmouth on the Isle of Wight, for example.

Yarmouth is a community of character with a harbour to match. Its salty, seamanlike atmosphere is an increasing rarity on the Solent. Moorings inside its old wooden wall are largely piles, where yachts and fishing boats secure fore and aft while the tide runs past them to fill the salt marshes upstream. In recent years a few walk-ashore marina berths have been built under a cloud of controversy, but the long, free-floating pontoon to which visitors raft up in merry conviviality is universally popular. Coming ashore requires a dinghy or, if this prospect fails to please, the wealthy or indolent can opt for a water taxi at a pound a head – rather more than the old Runcorn Ferry at 'tuppence per person per trip,' but convenient nonetheless.

To date, the harbour commissioners have resisted the demands of those who would plug into the mains and stroll into town no matter what the cost, and turned aside from the allure of the increased dues that would follow. They have realised that, just as MacDonalds' offering of what some might consider an acceptable burger is eroding the national character of dining across the globe, the marina is downgrading the planet's interesting ports to a homogeneous sameness.

The ancient and joyous haven of Yarmouth is currently a shining light in an English Channel where true quality of life is fast being eroded in favour of superficial comfort. To see it 'developed' into yet another caravan park would be a tragedy, so it came as a sharp shock for many to learn that the management of this Trust Port have apparently had a change of heart. Side-stepping the will of the majority of the diverse stakeholders, new plans show the whole harbour as, literally, a wall-to-wall marina.

It's one thing to rail against the dying of the light, but it's a lot more useful to find a way of switching it back on. The commissioners have taken a heavy barrage of flak over the way these proposals have been brought forward without consultation until very late in the day. Not even their legendary berthing staff were told until after the plans had been drawn up, but a ray of sunshine may yet cut through the gloom of this potential horror story. Rather than satisfying themselves by slagging off the forces of darkness, a group of level-headed residents are proposing alternative changes which could, if given proper consideration, satisfy most people's needs. If the commissioners can bring themselves to listen with open minds to such well-informed input, all may not yet be lost.

Sailors in the Solent will hold their breath. The rest of the nation should take more than a passing interest. This pestilence is a growing sickness that can infect us all; it would sow a seed of reason to report next year that Yarmouth, loved by so many, lives on.

JOIN THE CLUB

There's nothing like a good sailing yarn, even if
the truth has to be stretched a little

I f you're one of the majority that manages to avoid signing on as
'social secretary' for the local yacht club, spare the incumbent a
thought next time you settle down to enjoy the monthly speaker.
It's tough enough trying to entice decent lecturers to brave the snows
and address the Gasworks Creek Sailing Club, but when the treasurer's
budget is the thin side of a pound coin and no VAT, it's nigh-on
impossible.

It takes time to travel, and there's the talk to be written, so unless the
personality in question is salaried by a boss generous with his hours, it's
not unreasonable for him to reply, 'Delighted. The fee will be. . . .'

One noble exception to this rule was the late Tristan Jones. I was the
'soc sec' at the National Sailing Centre in Cowes back in his heyday, and
was shamefully briefed to invite the great man to address the students
for expenses only. To my astonishment he replied that he'd be there,
but he went on to point out that he lived in New York. Funding

37

transatlantic flights was not part of the Bursar's master-plan, so Jones' gamble paid off and we left him in peace to do what he did best.

Tristan Jones was a prolific writer of yachting narratives whose books have sold in quantities that are the envy of other nautical scribes. Beginning with the tale of his birth at sea in the vicinity of Tristan da Cunha, they go on to describe a life of adventure on the edge of the law. He tackles huge icebergs assisted only by a three-legged dog, faces down pirates and hard-nosed authorities with equal panache, and generally keeps his ships at sea against fearful odds. He also drags a small yacht across South America to sail on the highest navigable water in the world, Lake Titicaca. This exploit took place in the early 1970s and his book *The Impossible Voyage* was published shortly afterwards.

By coincidence, my wife and I trekked 12,500 feet up the Bolivian Andes at around the same time. Unaware of Jones' activities, we found Lake Titicaca and struck a deal to cruise these mystical waters with a fisherman. I still have the faded photographs. Shortly afterwards I read Jones' account to discover that, although his journey covered much of the same ground, we had clearly been travelling different planets.

As a budding journalist, this put me in an awkward position. On the one hand, we all must speak as we find. On the other, it didn't feel right to undermine one of the greats of my calling. As I digested the implications, I realised that I didn't care a hoot whether Tristan Jones was a hero or an exaggerator. A book has now been published with evidence proving that he was the latter, and I'm sorry it has. When failing health towards the end left him an amputee, he showed selfless courage in plenty. He inspired thousands and he entertained millions more. Above all, he was a storyteller, and the cool way he dealt with the only correspondence we ever shared leads me to suspect that deep down he didn't take himself too seriously. With all the certification and codes of practice which bombard us today, we are under considerable pressure to abandon our sense of proportion. We may not learn much about Yachtmastering from Tristan Jones, who considered wrestling an alligator more important than picking up a mooring, but he reminds us that seamen have traditionally kept their heads clear by seeing the joke.

Last week I made a business trip to the United States where chance led me to the mining settlement of Quartzsite Arizona. This half-horse town swelters in summer temperatures of over 100 degrees in a dusty desert surrounded by mountains from a Spaghetti Western. As I rounded the corner of the cracked clapboard shed fronting the burying ground, a sign over a batwing door announced implausibly that I had arrived at the Quartzsite Yacht Club. Shoving my way inside, I felt more than the usual nervousness associated with marching into someone else's club unannounced. The buzz of conversation switched off like a light bulb and a hush descended as the stewardess peered at me from behind a Coors Lite pump.

'Any chance of a beer? I'm a visiting yachtsman. . .' It sounded worse than lame, but I gave her the old 'Clint Eastwood' stare and hoped for the best. She eyed me up and down, then relaxed.

'Sure. Just hang any side arms by the door.'

I inspected the pegs provided. It was lunchtime and only three were in use. Reassured, I settled at the bar where I fell into conversation with a grizzled old miner who seemed to be a sort of rear commodore. He explained how the club came to be:

'California's next-door and they got earthquakes. Big time. When the whole goddam state finally falls into the Pacific Ocean, we'll have beach frontage here at Quartzsite. Real estate'll go sky high an' we'll be needin' a yacht club.'

His gaze didn't falter for a second and for my life I couldn't tell if he was winding me up, so I paid my subs to sign on as a 'charter member' just in case he was right. And if anyone thinks I'm shootin' the breeze, I have the burgee to prove it.

THE CLOCK IS TICKING

Are heaven and Earth to be sacrificed to satisfy some software engineer?

Like the rest of the pond life down here on Planet Earth, I'm grateful to Uncle Sam for launching his satellites so we can produce pin-point navigational accuracy with only the most rudimentary of skills. Despite this obligation to technology, however, I can't help feeling a deep sadness as my ocean sailing experience is impoverished in proportion to the benefits of GPS. Every year, I examine a number of candidates for the Ocean Yachtmaster certificate. Most have learned a smattering of celestial navigation in order to qualify. It's obvious from some of the results that there is no serious intent to pursue the art, and I understand why. The last time I crossed the Atlantic I only took my sextant out of the box once. In the dead of one remarkable night, the moon was pouring out enough light to give me a horizon, and there was the Pole Star shining through the blaze, low in the northern sky at the tail of the Little Bear. I knew my latitude without it, of course, but the extraordinary beauty of the scene demanded that I associate with my surroundings more profoundly than by merely staring at them.

By measuring the height of Polaris with my 1942 instrument, I had performed one of the greatest mysteries that has ever been available to Man. You don't have to be specially clever to manage the maths involved, and using the sextant is a simple skill that anyone with eyes and a steady hand can master, yet as I adjusted the micrometer and watched the image of the star kiss the edge of the moon-milky sea, I was in direct touch with the heavens. The body I was sighting on was of an immensity that dwarfs anything in our locality and, even as I watched, it was marching with unimaginable velocity away from me at a distance I cannot begin to comprehend. Sure, I can put numbers to such things, but once the digits have gone beyond our own experience, they are no more than rows of figures. I can't imagine a single light year, let alone hundreds, yet by connecting to such stars through my sextant I can fix my position to a mile or two on my tiny planet as it swims with its burning sisters around an unexceptional sun in a backwater galaxy.

We can still use celestial navigation, of course, and it's useful to run off a series of sun sights for an examination, but so long as we know where we are by courtesy of GPS, the magic will never be the same again. We can't turn back the clock, however. Electronics are here to stay, and I of all people realise this. So what's this column all about?

Astro navigation depends on the sun for the absolute time which is its life blood. 'No time, no longitude,' is the essential rule. When the issue of longitude was foremost in the minds of every mercantile nation, it just so happened that the problem was solved in England and that the Astronomer Royal had set up shop in Greenwich. The final arbiter of time had to be the Earth's relationship to the Heavens, and it was to their movements that everything was set. Inconveniently, the Earth doesn't spin at a perfect rate, so time was adjusted accordingly. It all came right again in about a year, so no problems were caused, and the navigation tables took it into account. Man needed time to run at an even rate for daily business, however, so the anomalies were ironed out into a 'mean' progress of the spheres. Because, for the purposes of navigational time, the day was measured from noon at Greenwich, the time standard became known as 'Greenwich Mean Time'. Not all the nations were thrilled about this name. France had hoped for the accolade, but the meridian of Greenwich was largely accepted as the 'prime' meridian from which longitude and time would be measured, and so things remained.

A century or three later, computers and their offspring were struggling to cope with any variations in the tick of the clock, and a super-precise measuring system took over from the sun. Every second, the Caesium 133 atom emanates precisely 9,192,631,770 oscillations of radiation at ground state. This became the universally accepted means of defining time. The name GMT was set aside in favour of Universal Time (UT), and loud was the cheering in Paris. Unfortunately for supporters of this otherwise perfect arrangement, our dear old Earth is slowing down. Not a lot, but enough to throw the atomic clocks out by a second or so every four years. So far, the answer has been to insert a 'leap second' on New Years Eve when needed, but now the wolves are howling to scrap the leap second and allow the official time of noon to drift steadily away from Greenwich. By my calculations, it will be in Paris in about 500 years, giving the French what they always wanted, before it drifts ever onwards into the wastes of Russia. The Americans like the idea; so do the Germans, the Italians and, of course, our neighbours across the Channel. We in Britain, however, are fighting to save not only Greenwich as the prime meridian, but also the concept of time – and hence our own little lives – being tied to the universal truth of the sun and stars. Never mind if a stand against the atoms upsets a few mobile phone and software companies. If a plebiscite were to be offered, I hope that all freeborn sailors, be they ancient or modern, will stand up and be counted.

LIFE IS LOOKING UP

When sailing at close quarters, don't forget to spare a glance for the masthead

I always feel sorry for people under sail in rivers who hit moored vessels. I know I shouldn't, because the victim of such an accident doesn't deserve such treatment, but we all must learn. If harbour-masters ban us from sailing for fun, we'll be far less confident when we are left with no option and playtime is a wistful memory.

My own boat still carries a vee-shaped dint in her teak taffrail from one hit-and-run driver, but I can't complain. Even though I'm too well-brought up to slink away after a collision, I haven't been blameless. My act of folly was a singular affair and at the time I was inclined to set it aside as bad luck, but I soon found out that luck at sea – be it bad or good – is generally of your own making. The collision I contrived to engineer might seem obscure, but if you are the sort of sailor who enjoys manoeuvring under canvas in tight quarters, you'll pull it off yourself one day if you don't watch out. Here's how it happens.

I was in my early years as an instructor aboard a Contessa 32, one of the world's most reliable and vice-free yachts. My students and I had spent the night at Bucklers Hard a couple of miles up the Beaulieu River on the Solent. Now we were bound back down after breakfast. It soon became apparent that we must beat most of the way to the sea. We could, of course, have motored, but on so sunny a morning that would have been a shame. The channel was wide enough for a Contessa to work to weather without straying into the well-spaced moorings at all, but the genoa was a big sail so we decided to minimise the number of tacks and use the full breadth of the river. Unlike many of her modern counterparts, the idea of such a yacht griping up in a gust among the moored craft was unthinkable. The skipper of the day was an ex-dinghy racer. We had everything possible in our favour.

Down towards the sea we beat, rattling the winches and scaring the ducks. The tide was helping us along, making the judgement calls interesting as we crabbed past yachts whose owners were doubtless earning a carefree crust up in the City. There was never the slightest chance we would touch anyone because we had a man on the bow calling the shots and the rest of us were near enough the stern for our own 'instant transits' to keep the aft end clear. So long as the boats we were approaching were moving relative to their background from both bow and stern, all was guaranteed to be well. There remained the possibility that a boat's bow might be closing one way and her stern the other, which would have meant a hit, but we were careful to avoid this and so our low-stress progress continued.

It was only as we shaped up to pass downstream of a lovely wooden yacht with a gentleman and his wife taking coffee in the cockpit that things turned unexpectedly pear-shaped. A goose parked on the sedge was disappearing smoothly behind the yacht's bow, and the bank behind her stern began to open as we swept by close to windward in the stiffening breeze. The gent smiled encouragingly, noting that we were well clear. Suddenly, his yacht heeled hard over and started to follow us down-river, the coffee pot hit the cockpit sole and his wife looked as if she had swallowed a cricket ball. Our helmsman was struggling to keep the Contessa from gybing round into the other boat, but he managed it and so the two boats staggered on, locked in this ghastly embrace, for what felt like a minute but was probably more like three seconds. We had, of course, hooked the gentleman's masthead with our topping lift which we had left trailing in a lubberly bight between its upper sheave and the boom end. Mercifully, it carried away before any worse damage was done.

There had been nothing wrong with our assessment about whether the boats themselves would collide, but nobody had thought to check aloft and we certainly had no masthead man sizing up the opposition. I ran back down to our victim and apologised. The couple were more understanding than I deserved, the damage appeared to be all ours, and we sailed home with a humbled young tutor trying to decide which was worse, ignorance or over-confidence.

I confessed my sins on returning to base and scored a well-deserved 'Nil Points' from my colleagues. Indeed, it seemed all the drinks were on me until our race training yacht arrived in from Lymington. The windex was bent at 90 degrees and there was a large gap where the anemometer should have been.

'What happened?' the boss asked the skipper.

'I was a good half boat's length from Jack in the Basket beacon; then I took a gust and wrapped up the stick. The wind instruments are still hanging on the topmark. Bit of bad luck really. . .'

GOOD, BECOMING POOR

Many a sailor suffers from a curious addiction imposed by the mercurial mandarins of the BBC

'Fair Isle, Faeroes and Southeast Iceland. . .'

I wish I'd a free breakfast for every drizzly morning I've crawled from a snug bunk before dawn, only to find my extra two minutes' snooze has consigned the local weather prognosis to history. The trouble with forecasts in this country is that they never seem to be broadcast when we want them. The dear old BBC is just one case in point. I love the Shipping Forecast ritual. Returning to home waters after protracted foreign voyages, the first, crackling strains of '*Sailing By*' and '*Rule Britannia*' reaching far out into the Atlantic bring tears to my eyes. It isn't long, though, before I am cursing with everyone else about the insane scheduling of some of these otherwise first-class bulletins. In harbour, the 0030 communiqué is patronised only by the supremely zealous and the hopeless drunk. At sea, it disturbs the peace of the middle watch when all except the lookout are trying to get some sleep. As for the 0535. . . Enough said.

My personal gripe is about the gratuitous manipulation of forecast times. For years, generations of British seafarers were subjected to *The Archers* while waiting for the 1355 bulletin. This stratagem led to widespread addiction, as was surely the BBC's intention. On the bridges of Her Majesty's destroyers, in frowzy fishing-vessel wheelhouses and around the cockpits of crack yachts, otherwise sane and courageous mariners 'listened in' daily to discover what bourgeois atrocity Linda Snell had perpetrated on honest Joe Grundy, and whether the influx of gay cricketers would give Sid Perks a stroke as he pulled pints of Shires in The Bull. So intense was this Archers-dependence that many of us took to enjoying our frugal sandwich during the afternoon episode before stiffening our upper lips for the ugly forecast that so often followed.

After getting us well and truly hooked, the Corporation arbitrarily moved the day-time forecast to noon on long wave only, and shoved the Ambridge visit back to 1403. For years, I had hung on, awaiting my lunch until the unnaturally late hour of 1340. Now, I must tighten my belt until after 1400. Worse to tell, unless I also switch on at noon, I miss the weather into the bargain. If you too are groaning beneath the emotional burden of this high-handed action, you are not alone.

Today's technology offers all manner of alternative access points to the Shipping Forecast, but at sea none of them really cut the mustard. Take Navtex, for example. A useful answer for those who've fitted one and remember to turn it on, but many of us don't have it. Broadband access to the various met sites is the ideal answer at home, but I doubt whether one yacht in ten manages an internet connection on the water. My own boat's hookup is expensive to run and not very reliable. Waiting for a download is like boiling a kettle over a candle.

Marinecall or the purveyors of SMS texts will charge me for the privilege, and half the time I can't get a mobile phone signal anyway. My 'moby' works almost without interruption along a thousand miles of mountainous Norwegian shore. It's fine in a comparatively poor country such as Portugal. Here in modern Britain, even my home mooring on the West Solent is in a black hole.

On the odd occasions when I brass up for the luxury of a marina berth, I might find a medium-term forecast on the dockmaster's board, but this won't help me in a remote anchorage in Scotland. Then there's VHF. Lovely, should you be listening when the nearest shore station repeats the Shipping Forecast every four hours. Unfortunately, the timing and the channels vary with each coastal zone. Sure, the relevant data are posted in the Almanac and the service is generally announced on Channel 16. The trouble is, as a peripatetic sort of skipper I often end up choosing the wrong channel from the selection recommended by the operator.

Over in America, none of this nonsense is tolerated. Instead, the National Oceanic and Atmospheric Administration (NOAA) operates two 24-hour VHF weather channels with rolling bulletins of around 10 minutes. As you sail down the coast and one channel begins to fade, you just switch to the other, and so on, all the way from Maine to Alaska. If you don't have a VHF, or you are a foreign 'alien' whose set does not have the US channels loaded, any corner store will sell you a dedicated 'weather radio'. I bought mine for fifteen bucks. Two AA batteries run it for months and it fits in my shirt pocket. The continuous information features a regularly updated five-day synopsis followed by a detailed, 48-hour local forecast of wind, precipitation, visibility and wave heights. You also get that most valuable of add-ons, a five-day planner. As you'd expect, small-craft weather advisories and general predictions of bad times are given their proper place. Reception never failed me in two years, and the service is absolutely free.

I wonder why we didn't think of it ourselves?

Don't take the times for granted. They change. Depressingly, even Rule Britannia has now been expungded by an ever-more politically correct BBC.

WINGED WONDERS

Sharing the sea with feathered friends is always an uplifting experience, unless there's a hungry French crew about

Birds have always been part of my seafaring. Some feign indifference to me, others note my passage with beady gaze. Many simply chum up, zooming along the shifting valleys of the waves, then soaring over the masthead. Perhaps they're sizing me up for a free meal if ever I'm careless enough to fall over the side; or maybe they're just curious about my gigantic wings and why I never manage to lift off. Who knows what goes on in their bird brains? But these are pelagic operators who only come ashore for a week or two annually for a bit of hunky-bunky and to pay the school fees. The land birds who happen by are a sorrier bunch altogether.

Once in a while a garden songster flutters on board. He looks lost and feeble, because he is. Unless he's a migrant on one of the feathery motorways of the sky, he has no business out there. Blown offshore, he is confused and desperate. Usually I try to give these chaps a decent breakfast, and generally encourage them as fellow warm-bloods. The trouble is, the sparrows and warblers nearly always end up ditching, which is terminal for them and depressing for me.

'It's only Nature's way,' I reassure myself, but I go below contemplating my own mortality.

Pigeons are a different kettle of fish altogether. Although landsmen to the core, they are proper long-distance flyers, and they've often taken a breather by flagging rides on my boats. One came to Norway, and a brace set up home on the foredeck of a large training yacht under my command halfway between Ushant and our destination in northern Spain. They lurked under the bulwarks as the hands tried to feed them on Quaker Oats and milk, but they turned up their beaks at these offerings. They'd arrived from the northeast and we reckoned they were on passage for Santander or Corunna, so when the mate got fed up with them fouling his scrubbed teak deck, we encouraged them to set course again. We pointed out the way, we shook a trail of crumbs across the deck towards the weather bow, we even tried launching them to windward, but they kept coming back. In the end we gave up, accepted them as shipmates, and signed them on as Ordinary Seabirds Pidge and Podge.

Twenty-four hours later a big, fast yacht overtook us, also bound towards Spain. As he came abeam, he broke out a massive French ensign and gave us a merry wave. O.S. Pidge hopped up onto the rail for a better view. Podge joined him. Together, they swayed to the roll for a few seconds having what appeared to be some sort of conference; then, without so much as a backward glance, they took off in a flurry of feathers and headed straight for 'John Francois'.

We watched our erstwhile shipmates through the binoculars as, without a morsel of shame, they circled the flying yacht, then landed on her deck. The French seemed to be fussing them up as they all disappeared over the horizon and we thought no more of the incident, except to log the birds as deserters.

Two days later, we anchored in a Spanish harbour beside the same Frenchman. The crew recognised us and one buzzed across in the Zodiac to invite us for drinks. After his third glass of petit Bordeaux, my mate asked the skipper what had happened to our pigeons.

The Breton spread out his hands with a gallic shrug and what must be described as a shifty mien.

'We did not know they were your birds.'

'They were stowaways. Did they fly on to Spain?'

'Mais non!' he looked mightily relieved. 'Our cook baked them in a tasty pie. . .'

On a lighter note, a couple of years back I was down at the famous dump on Martha's Vineyard, Massachusetts. Behind the skips stands a large shed where new or nearly-new items discarded by wealthy summer visitors are sorted by the thrifty locals. These islanders hate waste, and the shed is a sort of unofficial chandlery-cum-outfitter where all the goods are free to anyone who needs them. Fine clothing is hung on racks just like M&S, books are neatly stacked and hardware is carefully graded. On a back shelf I discovered a box stuffed with identical books about, of all things, European seabirds. I liberated these full-colour offerings, took one for my bunkside locker and have been dishing out the remainder to likely boats ever since. Don't write to claim your copy because there aren't many left and I don't want to be killed in the rush, but if your yacht does not have a bird book, treat yourself to a good one, even if you have to pay for it. Learning to recognise the locals as you plough the sea is an enriching experience that does not fade. And they aren't all pigeons.

GOOD, BAD, OR JUST UNLUCKY?

Sailing craft have their own character and some just can't stay out of trouble

Arthur White was a man who'd been involved with Thames sailing barges all his life. In 1947, he offered these words of wisdom to Nobby Clarke, an ex-RAF fighter pilot.

'Always make enquiries about a barge's character before you buy; it's much more important than the price.'

A barge, you might think, has no more character than the sum of her parts. However, before you write me off as a hopeless romantic, I'd urge you to read on, because the next quote is from Conor O'Brien, a 1930s dreadnought of the Southern Ocean – as hard-bitten a son of the sea as you'd meet in a month of cold winter days. He was referring to working sailing cutters built without formal plans. They were, he said, 'to the glory of natural man, who, living close to elemental things, develops an instinct for the earth or the sea which passes sophisticated understanding.'

So there we have it. Two sailors whose opinion only a fool would fail to respect, telling us that there's more to a boat than meets the eye. And we know it's true. Most of us have come across yachts that have never been anything but trouble. I remember one which a friend of mine commissioned from new. She was rammed twice on her mooring, then, one summer day, she was lying quietly at anchor when along came a large motorboat and drove straight into her cockpit. Next, she fell over when dried out alongside, and so her miseries compounded. She didn't even attract especially nice weather. In despair, my pal sold her and took on a different craft. Lo and Behold, the sun came out and, after several years trouble-free cruising, he concluded that the problem wasn't in him. It was his old boat that had been inherently wicked.

On the other side of the coin, I cruised a 1911 pilot cutter for 15 years that had every chance of delivering grief in sack-loads, yet she never did. She weighed in at 35 tons, measured 65 feet including her bowsprit and had a tiny engine with a spectacularly off-set propeller. Being young, I drove her around as though she was a modern fin-and-spade yacht, cramming her into tiny harbours and tackling voyages that made no concessions either to her extreme age or to what I'd politely refer to as her unrestored state. Yet in all that time the only major mishap she suffered was in the United States when a huge vessel smashed into her while she was anchored. That put her out of action for months, yet somehow she contrived her lay-up so that it coincided with the hurricane season. By the time she was fit for sea in late autumn, the only way to go was south to the Caribbean and so, constrained by her persuasive hand and fuelled with funds we'd scraped up in the meantime, my family and I enjoyed the loveliest winter's sailing we're ever likely to have. She'd been a lucky boat ever since she put her pilot aboard a high-paying ship on her delivery run to Barry from Fowey where she was built. She never lost that personality.

It's not all 'good' or 'bad', either. Character can be a matter of temperament. Some yachts make you feel secure and homely. Others are wet, wild and exciting. Some are inherently cheap to run. Others just can't help themselves and cost you a fortune year after year.

It could be said that this talk of soul only makes any sense with wooden boats that grew in the forest and which have been around long enough for a procession of mariners and events to leave their stamp in the timbers. An ancient house, after all, develops a 'feel' that's warm, cold, friendly, or downright spooky. What about production yachts, then? This can't apply to them, surely. Yet it does. The potential lies in every boat, and here's the crunch.

A boat is a lively thing which, if left alone, will drift free; she's a wild spirit, given half a chance, and as such, individuality is never far away. To refer to any yacht as 'it' is tacitly to deny this, and the practice robs us of some of the delight of ownership. 'She', or even 'he', indicates an acceptance of the mystic reality.

Government bureaucrats may have decreed a few years back that all ships are to be called, 'it'. Nelson's men knew better. So should we.

THE SACRED SOUND OF SILENCE

A reckless thespian shares his belief that there's a time for peace and quiet at sea

U nwanted noise comes our way in all sorts of packages. These days, one of the most infuriating sources is the gratuitous bleeping of electronic equipment, but more direct threats to serenity on board go back a lot further than this.

Many years ago I was moored on the inside of a raft of three boats on a town quay. The vessel immediately outside me was a 1930s motor-sailer of great character. Beyond her, a nondescript yacht had parked without shorelines. When I went on deck at sunset to lower my colours I found the motor-sailer man doing the same. I thought I recognised his chiselled profile and air of artistic sensibility, but instead of the smoking jacket that might have been appropriate, he was sporting a 'Noel Coward' dressing gown. The newly lit dockside arc lights glinted off its rich silk reveres as he graciously offered me a sundowner. He was a famous actor, cruising the Channel with his aged father while resting between parts. The old gentleman, it turned out, had survived the whole of WWI at sea with the Royal Navy before achieving some remarkable yachting exploits so long ago that Hitler and his gang were still limbering up.

As night fell and the traffic thinned away, peace descended on the scene until the yacht outside us both fired up her engine, presumably to charge her batteries. I never discovered how this ill-starred machine pushed the boat along, but it was spectacular for noise and fumes. Mr Motor-sailer senior left off recounting the details of a near-sinking in a 1930s Bermuda Race to give the yacht's owner a steely stare, but the man sat stolidly in his cockpit and refused all eye contact. The unwritten law, of course, then as now, is that if you haven't managed to bang your power up by sunset, you either light your oil lamps or sit in the dark and resolve to do better next time. To make somebody else's evening hideous in order to chill a fridge was never acceptable in civilized circles, but whatever our neighbour's reasons, he was oblivious to the unpleasantness his zeal for volts was visiting on the rest of us.

We continued to sip our cocktails and nothing was said directly for about 15 minutes. Then the actor set his tumbler down on the cockpit table and rose magnificently to his feet, squaring that paisley dressing gown across his noble shoulders.

'I expect this fellow could do with some assistance, Father,' he said, stepping up onto his scrubbed deck. Ignoring the outside skipper who was still lurking in his cockpit, he quietly let go the yacht's lines. As the last one was tossed aboard and the boat drifted away towards the sea, the noise-maker seemed finally to realise what was happening.

'What the devil are you playing at?' he roared as an initially bemused look gave way to rage.

'I could hear you warming up your motor, old boy,' replied our hero in a cut-glass accent. 'You were obviously about to leave. I just wanted to give you a hand.'

Unfriendly engine-running in today's harbours isn't only about charging batteries. That at least is a direct affront. Far worse is the creeping stealth of those 'safe' electric boat cookers which require a gen-erator to be flashed up before the owner's wife can brew her morning tea. Safe their cookers may be, but such yachts often feature plug-in kettles. The last time I was shipmates with one of these, it fell off the galley top at sea and scalded the cook. It all depends on what you mean by 'safe', I suppose, but there is no escaping the antisocial aspects of electric cookers in harbour.

I didn't actually set out to write about battery charging out of hours but, as any novelist will tell you, words have a way of taking over a writer's mind. Rather than entering a discussion about whether the thought is father to the word or vice-versa, I'll return to my original theme of those dismal bleeps which make our cabins sound like supermarket checkouts with every finger-stroke on GPS units, radio sets and the rest.

I finally ran out of patience with these when a much-needed watch below was repeatedly disturbed by a new GPS receiver announcing – just because it could – that we had arrived at some waypoint or other. One of my greatest moments of liberation came when all my efforts to defuse this horror had failed and I resorted to the book of instructions. In tiny print right at the back was a line in italics – *To silence sound signal enter setup scroll mute enter*. It demanded a serious effort of will not to heave this gobbledegook out the porthole, but as soon as I did what the manual was trying to say, tranquillity was restored and I felt the sort of triumph Archimedes must have enjoyed when his bath slopped over.

Now, all I have to do is deduce a global method for gagging that most irritating of all improvements, the universal echo-sounder depth alarm.

TESTING TIMES

It makes sense to try before you buy, though going aground was not in the passage plan

When I bought my original cruising boat, her owner took me for a trial sail. He was a sportsman himself and had assessed me as a man who enjoys driving a vessel to her limits. It was blowing Force 6, so with giant headsails and not a reef to be seen we had a rough time of it, but he made his point. Nothing broke and I'd already fallen in love. Hoping that she wouldn't always sail with her lee rail inches below the water, I signed the papers.

I don't know what it was about that yacht, but a similar thing happened when a potential buyer showed up for a trip out five years later. My wife and I were selling because she was eight months pregnant and our lovely craft was not going to accommodate three. I advertised in *YM* and two customers nibbled at my hook. The first had never sailed a gaffer before and wanted the experience before paying for a survey. I realise now that this was upside down, but it seemed sensible enough then, so we agreed a date.

Our man arrived on the dock one windy spring morning. He didn't come alone as I had done. He brought his wife, a friend and an aged aunt. They crashed aboard at Lymington Yacht Haven, struggling with a hefty wicker hamper containing lunch, so the day seemed filled with promise. The yacht, however, had other ideas.

Because it was blowing like a banshee I'd bent on the storm jib. This tiny sail sets from the bowsprit end and is vital to balance a gaff cutter. Off the wind, she may sail with staysail and main; to windward, without a jib she walks with a pronounced limp. Somehow, this sail must have escaped the attentions of my sailmaker's valeting program because it featured a galvanised luff wire which turned out to be well past its prime. No sooner was it hoisted than it carried away near the head, leaving the halyard block flailing aloft and the rest of the sail dredging for oysters.

I was fit in those days, so I hove to, grappled in the remains, then nipped up the mast in short order to retrieve the block. Mrs Buyer was looking on aghast, as Hubbie, while far better heeled than yours truly, was not a 30-year-old who'd just completed three years full-time cruising. As predicted, with nothing on the bowsprit the boat sailed like a pig, so I roused out the Number Two, set it in a frightening thunder of canvas, and away we went with my old friend the lee rail as far under as it had been on my own trial sail.

Over-pressed, we were not making well to weather, and the Spring flood eventually carried us a mile downtide of Lymington. To disguise this sorry performance I suggested starting the engine. The ladies agreed with obvious relief, so down came the sails and on went the Volvo, which ran like a trooper until halfway back up the river. Just as the Isle of Wight ferry was upon us, it showed what it thought of the day's events by dying, with every sign of refusal to return to service without the attentions of a marine engineer.

Normally, I'm unfazed by engine failure. Whip up some rag and away we go, is my maxim. Unfortunately, the ferry's displacement wave took so much water that we went hugely aground. We lay hard over amid screams of woe and terror, and ended up well stuffed in the mud on the lee shore.

I carried out a kedge with the dinghy and prepared to wait patiently for the tide. My wife suggested to The Quality that this might be just the moment to break open the hamper, but instead of this tempting proposition, the aunt demanded we call the coastguard for assistance. This nonsense was mercifully avoided because we had no VHF and, sure enough, an hour later we floated off. I made sail and my wife steered us up to the anchor, tack for tack, as she'd done many times before although, as she later reminded me, not when about to give birth. We thrashed clear of the ooze and luffed off the last of our way alongside the Royal Lymington pontoon where a bosun with an eye for a good laugh took our lines. The buyers couldn't get ashore quickly enough. We never saw them again.

The next person to view the ship understood what he was buying just by looking at her, and he wrote the cheque on the saloon table there and then. The boat approved. She was partial to people who knew their own minds.

Rather like the Three Bears' porridge, that first cruiser was sold because she was no longer big enough. I parted company with her 35-ton successor nearly 20 years later for the opposite reason. The yacht I have today is just right. She's taken us far and wide in comfort and security for more than a decade, but all things come to pass. I've owned nothing but gaffers since I was a lad and although I've sailed three-cornered boats on many a day when the dog wouldn't sail, I've never had one to call my own. It's time to take the plunge into a new challenge.

Don't ask what'll come next, and Heaven only knows what sort of trials will mark the transfer, but a change is as good as a rest. I just hope none of my customers turn up with hampers.

ALWAYS READ THE LABEL

The tragic passing of an age-old preservative
and a resounding toast to Darwin

D on't you just love the scent of Stockholm Tar wafting to leeward as a traditional boat sails by? I use it mixed with boiled
linseed oil to slush down the galvanised shrouds and stays of
my gaff cutter, and I'm doing far more than protecting my investment.
I'm giving the neighbours an olfactory treat and connecting myself with
generations of seamen stretching back to biblical times. That smell has
always defined the aura of working ships: North Sea smacks sailing after
shoals of herring, clippers driving up the South Atlantic with tea from
China, the *Revenge* standing out to harry the Armada, the Vikings and,
for all I know, the Greek triremes thrashing the Persians at Salamis.
They all chose this natural product to protect, rejuvenate and lubricate
their rigging. It also works wonders for wood and, apparently, horses'
hooves.

Stockholm Tar is made by some mysterious technique involving
boiling up the roots of pine trees, and a little goes a long way. I still
haven't finished the last of a large plastic jerry I bought in Bergen in

1983. It's just as well I grabbed so much while I could because – guess what – for our safety, comfort and no doubt convenience as well, this time-honoured unction is about to be banned. In an office in Brussels, the biocide section of the Environmental Directorate has decided it is so toxic that it represents a serious risk to the environment and the lives of people coming into contact with it.

I suppose if you were to pour five gallons of Stockholm Tar down the nearest drain it might create damage on a similar scale to the contents of a lorry sump and I don't doubt that imbibing a regular tumbler-full would do you no good. We live in enlightened times, however, and most people now know that discarding used lubricant indiscriminately is a criminal offence. Many oil cans even feature useful advice against drinking the stuff. So far, I haven't seen a Stockholm Tar container carrying a government health warning. This is probably because it's used in comparatively small amounts, it's expensive, so nobody would think of dumping it, and anyone sufficiently barking mad as to slurp it or rub it under their armpits is probably better taken out of the gene pool.

The officials have generously decided that a couple of established applications are OK. In no particular order, these are women's makeup and food colouring. At the time of writing the Finns and Norwegians are having a rough ride trying to negotiate a third dispensation to go on treating wooden churches with it, some of which have lasted a thousand years with no other preservative.

If you sail a modern yacht, you probably have more important things to lobby your MP about than this particular piece of silliness, but we sailors do need to grumble rather more loudly. Earlier this year I happened by a boat on the hard whose wooden mast was surrounded by scaffolding. I expect the solitary figure working aloft was very healthy and extraordinarily safe, but I dread to think what the owner was having to pay to be so solicitous of his welfare. After 230 years or so, the chaps who service the rigging of HMS *Victory* are no longer allowed to climb the ratlines because it's been decided that the practice is unsafe. Instead they are carried skywards by cherry-picker cranes at a cost I'd rather not contemplate. My local Old Gaffers' race committee is supposed to produce a written risk assessment before an annual event that has been managed without disaster for 40 years, and so the list goes on.

Nobody would deny that safety standards have progressed to everyone's benefit since World War II. Compared with their unspeakable predecessors, modern, easy-to-wear lifejackets have done a huge amount to encourage people to slip them on. I can almost literally lose my 21st century small-tube radar reflector aloft instead of suffering the windage and hateful ugliness of what went before. These are among many genuine improvements whose best aspect is that we have somehow retained the freedom to choose when and whether to use them. It's the erosion of our liberty by nonsensical regulations that we must fight.

Left to ourselves, we generally make the right decisions. It's not so very long since a campaign was mounted to encourage yachtsmen to wear hard hats following one unlucky individual being killed when the boat gybed all standing. The absence of these unlikely aids to eternal life in our oilskin lockers pays mute tribute to our collective common sense. If everything in the world is to be legislated, labelled and imposed on us by people who understand little of the real problems we face, we'll end up not trusting our own judgement. Then I'll be in dire danger from my pre-Health-and-Safety jerry-can:

'Shot of Stockholm Tar in your gin, Skipper?'

'Nothing on the label says I shouldn't. Cheers!'

Another triumph for Natural Selection.

WHERE'S WALLANDER?

Journeying by sea presents opportunities that are beyond the reach of those restricted to land

The more that human activity becomes regulated, the happier I am to be a sailor. The feeling of independence once the shorelines are slipped is one of the core delights of cruising. That, and the ever-present lure of the unknown. All of us who go to sea are adventurers at heart, seeking the unexpected in a world where almost everything else is pre-ordained – from what time it will rain in three days, to the number of 'miles to next service' on the car's LED display. We are designed to cope with uncertainty, and dealing with it delivers more than its share of job satisfaction. And it isn't all about emergencies. The upside is that landfall on a strange coast can produce unscheduled sources of satisfaction.

My first visit to the southern states of America came when I arrived in a modest boat from the West Indies. I'd left the Virgin Islands in late March so it was very early in the season. This and the resultant morning frosts probably kept the crowds away, and I found an unspoilt wonderland of nature. My engine was on the skids as usual, so I ghosted through the limpid, peaty water of the Carolina Cypress swamps in silence. Later, I rollicked across the wide sounds of Pamlico and Albemarle, bound for the Outer Banks with their sparse populations and flocks of birds. I didn't need Dvorak, a concert hall and the New World Symphony. The music was thundering in my head. I was seeing America as the first settlers must have seen it and I was transfixed. Many years later, I visited the old haunts, this time from the land in a rental car. To approach anywhere near the wilderness, vast deserts of man-made mediocrity had to be traversed. Motorways, gas stations, hamburger stands and lawyers' offices lay between me and what, for all I knew, was the fairytale country I'd once travelled, but I couldn't recapture that moment. The sea was the only way.

As well as the joys of nature, turning up somewhere by boat can often lead one to the best parties in town. If, like me, you find yourself tuning in to the morose Swedish detective Wallander on late-night TV, you'll be intimate by now with the provincial, south-coast port of Ystad. Unlike the community represented in Midsomer Murders, which must by now be measurably down in population on account of the toll taken by the unlawful killings, Ystad is a real place. I sailed into it one sunny day a couple of summers ago and, striking out into town from the lovely sandy marina with its boardwalks and busy little cafes, I discovered one of the finest chandleries in Europe. They sold everything a modern yacht needs, but they also specialised in all the goods required to keep a serious sailing ship at sea. They even purveyed seamen's primitive art of the highest calibre. The place smelt of Stockholm tar, hemp and linseed oil. It was like heaven. I might mention as an aside that even this remarkable emporium featured in a recent episode of Wallander, although the staff had been changed to suit the demands of the Swedish Actors' Union. Instead of the highly civilized lady who had served me with a ball of tarred marline and a mooring spring, a shifty-looking character lurking in the gloomy recesses behind the fenders refused to give the honest guardians of the law a straight answer. Thank goodness he wasn't there when I showed up. Instead, the real chandler told me about the 18th century opera house the town had just refurbished. That night was the grand-opening, featuring an agenda of pure Mozart. I galloped up to the box office, secured the last two tickets and nipped back to the ship for the blazer and ducks. My wife shook out her best dress and we passed an evening of pure delight next to an elderly Swede in a pink dinner jacket.

We didn't see Wallander around. Neither did the guys we met the next day who'd arrived by motor home. They'd also missed the opera. Not having fetched up by sea, they hadn't visited the chandlery, so they didn't know it was on.

WEATHER OR NOT

Sailors are faced with constant choices - but one thing they'll never be able to choose is the weather

I t'll soon be Christmas. My boat's safely tucked up in the river and I'm sitting by the bogey stove searching my soul about how to hoist this year's festive tree to the masthead without graunching the varnish. There are two choices of halyard. Either abaft the spar on the main topsail, or forward on the 'jib-top'. I open up the fire, dodge the usual puff of smoke and toss on another chunk of driftwood. Then I sit back and chuckle. If only all decisions were that simple! Here's one we often face when we're cruising, and it's a real killer.

You're stuck in a harbour somewhere in Northern France. Time is running out and the weather has been rubbish for days. Home lies an ugly 80 miles to windward. You've exhausted the pleasures of the Bar du Port and the local restaurateur is beginning to think you fancy him. The harbourmaster rubs his hands in glee as you totter into his lair to brass up for yet another day, and that benighted northeaster keeps on blowing its socks off. Nobody but an idiot would put to sea. Or would they?

The morning forecast on the board outside the Capitainerie is promising 'Force 4 to 6, occasionally 7'. A fat lot of use that is. You could live with four, even on the nose. Six you don't want at all, and seven will land you in the divorce court with no witnesses on your side. The usual group of bedraggled fellow-prisoners has clustered around the bulletin.

'What do you think, then?' asks your new friend from berth C45.

'I'm in no rush. I'm going to sit tight,' interjects the man from the steel 50-footer that's so big and powerful he could go any time he wanted.

'I really need to get back, but I don't want to put the kids off,' says Jemima, whose husband's morale has collapsed so completely that he's still in his bunk.

'Well,' you announce, grasping the nettle painfully by the thick part of the stem, 'I'm under the cosh to leave and the breeze does seem to be taking off a bit. Maybe we'll get more four than six today. I'm going to give it a go.'

Ever the optimist, you slip your lines. A few white faces peer out from companionways and one bold spirit gives you a wave. As you motor past the lighthouse a mean-looking gust with rain on its breath blackens the water, but you convince yourself that it's only 'piping up around the headland.' Hoisting the main is no fun because of the seas bouncing back off the harbour wall, and for the moment you can't face the drama of unrolling enough genoa to power the boat, so you stick with main and motor. Half an hour out, the wind has settled into a solid Force 6 and you're unable to lay within 30 degrees of home, even motorsailing. The boat falls off a square wave and buries her foredeck into a hole big enough to garage a corporation bus. The whole rig shudders, the engine slows momentarily and your heart falters. Perhaps you should have stayed put with the faint-hearts. The trouble is, what do you do now?

Deep down, you know that the correct response is to admit you were wrong and go back in, but the Devil is whining in your ear that you'd be gutless. Also, you'll have to face up to the inquisition on the dock. Asking the crew outright is probably not a good idea because, whatever you do in the end, the last thing you want in these conditions is dissenters. This is one of those decisions for which, as Johnny Cash remarked, 'You're gonna walk that lonesome valley by yourself.'

Perhaps if you muscle it out for another couple of hours everyone will be pleased you did. After all, some of the best memories come from bad experiences. Momentarily, the wind falters and eases to 20 knots, but it's only fooling with you. The next time it pipes up it hits 28 knots and one of the crew throws up. Home is looking further and further away and suddenly it's all too much. You finally accept that today is a bust and turn around.

Back in harbour, you make a brave face of it with your pals. Mercifully, the weather-man is now offering a better deal tomorrow, so you book in for dinner one last time, and quietly congratulate yourself.

Anyone can judge decisions with the wisdom of hindsight, but when it comes to the sea, the weather is the mainspring of the whole business and sailors have been second-guessing it since the dawn of history. As long as we make diligent efforts to gather all the data available we can do no more. The decision was right when we made it. It just turned out wrong. There's no point in self-flagellation. The world keeps on turning, and in the end it's the action we take to sort it all out that counts.

As for me and my Christmas tree problem, the wind's flipped round into the north and strengthened. I'm head-up to the northeast, so if I go for the jib-top the foliage will scrape as I pull it up. The main topsail halyard it is, then. The tree'll blow off from the mast all the way before I belay it to give Santa a beacon to steer for. That's the theory anyway. Happy Christmas!

WRESTLING THE PYTHON OF MODERNITY

The latest yachts may boast convenience but are they really set up for sailing?

S winging down the pontoons nearest the shore at the recent Southampton Boat Show, my first impressions were a delight. The Irish replica emigrant ship *Jeanie Johnston* was an inspiration, while Pete Goss's harmonious lugger showed an old-fashioned British sense of adventure as well as some decent respect for sailors from another time; fishermen who knew full well what the sea could do, yet still sailed an open boat to Australia to join the gold rush. As I strolled on, however, I found myself losing the will to live. Many of the new yachts shamelessly paraded grossly fat sterns whose lack of proportion could promise nothing but hours of misery at the helm in gusty conditions, and there was a proliferation of kit for kidding us that we're in a house and not at sea at all that I found especially inappropriate.

'You'll find the yacht has every comfort, but no luxury,' explained the wise old owner of a notably basic vessel I once bought. Six months and a couple of major ocean gales later, I knew what he meant. The boat's seakindly hull and snug accommodation made her a joy on passage. She lacked a deep freeze, double bunks fore and aft, electric heads and complex radio equipment for talking to my friends if I felt lonely, but she had a lovely motion and massive water tanks.

Not long ago I was crossing the Atlantic with a friend when his water maker packed up. Demand for water was heavy and tankage less generous than it might have been without the machine. Even the power-driven heads were flushed by fresh water. Jolly nice too, in some ways, but no good if there isn't enough in the tanks to do the necessary. Carting buckets of clean sea through my private 'en suite' brought a new dimension to the term 'flushed with success'. When we eventually filled up alongside a tropical pier swarming with cockroaches, I was no longer in any doubt about how useful self-sufficiency can be.

Never having shipped much in the way of technology, I have managed to avoid becoming a prisoner of my own systems waiting for spares in far-off lands. On the other hand, with no water maker, I've had to tank up in some extreme spots. Possibly my worst fill ever was in Iceland, on a yacht whose inspired designer had sited the standard-sized deck fitting in the middle of the saloon table. This worked adequately in a clean marina with a small pipe and a controllable tap nearby. Secured among the Reykjavik fishing boats it was a different story. The only source was the harbour board's fire hose. This was long enough to reach across the five boats inside us, but turning it on had to be left to a policeman enjoying a smoke beside the wheel valve. The canvas piping had the bore and consistency of a dead python, and as we fed the mighty brass nozzle down the companionway we suspected we might be in for trouble.

'Tell him to turn it on gently,' I advised the mate, who was climbing onto our neighbour's wheelhouse to communicate with the cop. I stationed myself in the cockpit to call the shots while the cook held the hose in place and waited. I heard the mate shout something along the lines of, 'OK. Let's have it.' The hose kicked a couple of times, then went as stiff as a drainpipe and slammed me against the coaming. From below came a scream followed by a noise normally only heard at waterfalls. Diving down the steps, I found the cook clinging grimly onto the nozzle, apparently possessed of a demon. The hose was flicking her around the cabin like a rag doll while jetting hundreds of gallons of Iceland's purest over the cushions, books, charts, and everything else in reach.

If we'd had a water maker, of course, we would have been spared all this. Secure in the knowledge that capacity was not an issue, we'd also have showered every day, rejoiced in regular clean underwear and been generally happier sailors. The downside is the lurking spectre of failure when you least want it. Given average rainfall potential, however, a different solution may appeal to lateral thinkers.

Being children of civilization, we tend to regard drinking water as originating from pipes on shore, forgetting that the stuff really falls to us straight from the sky at the popular price. I used to cross oceans with my wife on a boat that carried only 40 gallons. We were once six weeks at sea in the tropics, yet still arrived with our tanks over half full. The secret wasn't not washing, it was never wasting a squall. We'd let the rain rinse the mainsail for a couple of minutes, then hang a bucket under the gooseneck. It filled in no time, we tipped the contents down the spout and went round again. I always envied better set-up yachts that had water catchers integral with their sun awnings, but my favourite arrangement is on a simple steel cruiser designed, built and owned by an unsung hero of the deep, Nick Skeates.

Nick's fillers are immediately inboard of the toerails at the lowest point of the sheer. All he has to do is wait for a good downpour, block up the scuppers with tailor-made bungs, open the caps and sit back. Self-sufficiency, with no membranes to clog and no pumps to fail. It's a far cry from the Southampton Boat Show, but in times when cash is hard to find it's bit like a decent sea berth – a lot more use on board than a gigantic double bed without leeboards.

TOUCHING THE BOTTOM

A windswept Scottish anchorage teaches important lessons in home comforts and never being too sure of yourself

I once asked an elderly yachtsman who had sailed from the same river all his life whether he ever got bored. His reply showed the question to be profoundly inappropriate.

'How could I be bored?' he said. 'The landscape might not change much, but the water's what it's about. Every day is different.'

I was reminded of this while on a pilgrimage to the Hebrides in my old pilot cutter *Hirta*. I'd sailed her north from the Solent with a mind to visiting St Kilda. Half a day to the westward of the Sound of Harris, the main island of this remote group bears the same name as the one given to the boat in the 1930s by the man who owned them both.

Typically for those bound towards the only roadstead, Village Bay, we were stopped in our tracks by gales ripping down from Iceland. We limped back into Loch Portain on North Uist where we found a quiet hole by a small post office. The chart showed a flattish area with widely spaced soundings, so I anchored at low water in 12 feet on the dial, laid out a hefty length of cable and kissed my troubles goodbye.

After three days of damp, freezing weather, we were running low on coal for our bogey stove, so I rowed ashore to strike a deal with the post mistress, whose neat stack of turf had caught my eye.

'Any chance of buying some peat for my fire?' I dripped shamelessly on her clean boards.

'None whatsoever.'

Sadly, I opened the door onto the driving drizzle, but as the wind grabbed the brim of my sou'wester, she called me back with a twinkle.

'You can help yourself to all you can carry, though. . .'

I loaded up a canvas sack, bought a pair of huge and hairy socks knitted before my very eyes by this generous lady's old mum, then pulled home to stoke up. The following day the wind was still howling, but overnight the moon had been waxing big above the driving wrack. As the tide came in towards teatime, far more land was disappearing than previously, and instead of high water bringing a depth of 18ft, we were finding 22. I went forward to check the cable at sunset and saw the half-inch chain standing out bar-taut in front of the boat. Dragging her 120lb Fisherman was not one of the boat's bad habits, but to sleep more easily I surged out another 10 fathoms, giving her a scope of nine to one. The holding ground had proved itself already and we could now have ridden out a hurricane except that the changing scene was not confined to the top of the tide. When I rose at 0800 for a healing brew, it was blowing harder than ever, and by coffee time, the beach was showing more of its bones than I wanted to see. *Hirta* was still where she had been – my transits confirmed that beyond doubt – but by the bottom of the tide we had only a foot under our keel and the tides were still building.

We bumped that midnight. Not severely, but the thud left no doubt we'd have to shift berth at first light, come storm or tempest. As things fell out, the issue never arose because the Clerk of the Weather generously switched off the westerly gale. Instead of the spell of moderate northerlies we might have expected, however, he replaced it with a stiff east wind which would be blowing straight into Village Bay with a 40-mile fetch. We submitted to fate, built up the fire and beat back across a confused Minch towards Skye, contemplating the lessons learned.

The first message was the inestimable benefit of a real stove. If we'd had blown-air heating, I'd never have met the post mistress and her matchless mother, my feet would have been less snug for the remainder of the cruise and I'd have burned up valuable diesel. The batteries would also have taken a needless drain. The second, perhaps more important point, was that examining charted depths in detail would not have made any difference to the fact that my chosen spot to anchor ultimately turned dodgy. I selected it on sounder alone, reckoning that all I needed was enough water to float me. Had it been half-tide instead of low tide, I'd only have needed to check my tidal curve to see how much it would fall between anchoring time and low water, add that to my draught plus a clearance figure and let go. Easy. I always suspect a Yachtmaster candidate who looks too closely at soundings and adds them into the equation of his depth calculation for anchoring overnight. After all, there's no certainty that the sounding you are nailing your colours to is exactly where you'd like to think it is, especially if you're using an over-zoomed chart plotter! The sounder should be telling the whole truth and nothing but the truth.

My plan had worked well. The mistake was to reckon without a long wait and to forget that in a tidal anchorage, just as in my old friend's river, no two days are ever quite the same.

DEAD CERT

Compulsory certification shouldn't rob a sailor of his right to drown himself – nor will it raise standards of seamanship

I t's many years now since a couple of shipmates and I went to sea with Commander Bill Anderson to be assessed as potential Yachtmaster Examiners. Bill had only recently piloted the RYA scheme out of the dark ages into the world's leading qualification system. It was mid-winter and our boat was an unheated cruiser-racer that threw icy water around like the firehose on a London River tugboat. Our vintage oilskins gave only nominal protection, so by turn-in time on 'Day One' we were saturated and very cold indeed.

I was occupying a saloon settee directly beneath Bill, who had sportingly volunteered for the pilot berth. This wretched platform boasted the proportions of a bookshelf so mean it would have struggled to support a decent almanac, and the miserable incumbent's only hope of relief from the dripping condensation was when it froze to the deckhead around midnight.

Possibly because of the biting frost stiffening my five-quid sleeping bag, I wasn't having much luck nodding off. I realised Bill was experiencing similar difficulties when a match flared up in the corner followed by a cloud of aromatic pipe smoke. Here, I thought, was a chance to pick up a few nuggets from the great man, so I asked him the question that has since been posed to me more times than I can number.

'What do you think, Bill, ' I ventured, 'about compulsory certification for sailors?'

Anderson's reply was a distillation of the wisdom for which he remains famous.

'It's sensible to set standards for anyone accepting other people's money for taking them to sea. The customers may not be qualified to judge the boat or the skipper, and the innocent deserve some protection. The way things are going, that'll come into the rules soon and we shouldn't oppose it.' His pipe glowed in the dark cabin. Then he chuckled. 'What we must fight for is the private British sailor's right to drown himself, his family and his friends however he chooses. If we bring in a driving test for everyone, it'll inevitably be pitched below Day Skipper level. People will pass too easily and it's only human nature that many will decide there's nothing more to it – as most do on the roads. So long as we hold onto the right to police ourselves, a few will always do nothing, but many will strive for higher things. That's the way we'll raise standards.'

History has proved him royally correct and the battle is still not lost. The Germans now must submit to examination, whether or not they intend operating commercially. Others on the continent are teetering on the brink. Entirely through the efforts of Bill Anderson and his successors, we on the 'Sceptred Isle' still retain the option.

When it comes to boats, the certification issue is rather different. The European Recreational Craft Directive (RCD) continues to chisel away at our freedom of choice. We can only be thankful that the RYA's technical team are keeping it in some sort of check, because this deplorable initiative shows how vital it is to fight tooth and nail for the voluntary status of the Yachtmaster scheme. Selecting the RCD from your bunkside locker doesn't compare for entertainment value with *A Dodgy Night at Pompey Lil's*, but it does become interesting when you arrive at the bit about standards of construction and stability. Leafing through the pages, however, one can't help reflecting that what counts at sea are those things that really do happen, rather than what the regulations say ought to happen. If the *Saucy Sal* doesn't measure up to some formula but keeps getting away with it, while *Supersailer.com* ticks all the boxes but cops it as soon as the big seas roll, you have to wonder why. Perhaps it's because the crew of *Supersailer.com* aren't fit to be in charge of a rowing boat, while *Saucy Sal*'s crowd are prime seamen who could navigate safely in a sieve. Maybe *Saucy Sal* is plain lucky while *Supersailer* is not, but perhaps the truth lies in which questions are being asked. Fortunately, British citizens with pre-June 1998 vessels can still do as they please within the limits of common sense and the laws of the sea. In the current climate of knee-jerk legislation for every mishap, thank goodness these are rarely flouted.

There was no soul-searching about certificates in pre-RCD days. Many years back, I shipped with a well-respected elderly yachtsman who took young folk to sea in an ancient working craft. Her transom planking was so rotten that a board literally fell off it in Holland.

'Never mind my dears,' he said, 'We'll nail this useful plastic bag over the hole and fix her up somewhere else. We'll be close-hauled all the way home, so there'll be no pressure on the stern.'

He was absolutely right. He sailed sensibly and we fetched the Hamble late but safe. That plastic bag became notorious as he made the trip again and again, bringing joy, laughter and a lively sense of their own mortality to a generation of sailors.

Twenty years after my old skipper went peacefully to his final survey, his yacht is still sailing the seas he taught so many to love. She's as innocent of the RCD as the day she was launched, and he never did pass his Yachtmaster exam.

SPRING FEVER

Keep an eye on the wind but ignore the moon and sun at your peril, for the sea will always surprise the sailor

'A neap-tide of work, then a spring of liquor.' So the Irish poet Richard Murphy described the life of the owner of the last Galway fishing hooker, the *Ave Maria*. Having just returned from cruising the English Channel that I know so well, I can't fault the man's powers of observation. The same pattern of existence must have been the lot of the pêcheurs of Brittany, working the sardine shoals from their open luggers in the days before engines finally made them the masters of the sea.

The French have a name for spring tides. 'Vives-eaux' they call them. Living waters. Neaps are 'Mortes-eaux', as dead as dead can be – so much more descriptive than our bland, English terminology. With the sea alive and your home patch a mass of rocks that cover and uncover twice a day, you can't fight it in a vernacular sailing boat with no engine, so you may as well give up and inspect the level in your favourite bottle

79

instead. When the currents are lifeless and the low waters high, that's the time to fill your nets and top up your bank account to see you over the next rough patch as the moon waxes and the streams begin to rumble.

One thing the sea reminds me about each summer is that I, for one, am never too old to learn. I've always preferred anchoring to the ever-increasing bills in marinas, to say nothing of the peace it can bring. Despite the proliferation of organised berthing and locks to cheat the tide, there are still plenty of places to drop the hook. Indeed, my pal Dutch Rob spent a whole summer in the Channel not so long ago and never once paid a harbourmaster. His ground tackle did the work most of us leave to our cheque books. The problem with this policy is spring tides, especially down in the Channel Islands and the waters around St Malo. Here, ranges of 40 feet and more are not unusual, so you need a lot of cable at the top of the tide, and a lot of space between you and the shore if you're hoping to be afloat when it's all gone away. I don't mind the depth, because I have a good windlass and loads of chain. It's the low water that's the challenge.

At dead neaps a boat drawing six feet can often anchor right up on the green sections of the chart, so 'high' is the level of low water. This allows you to tuck in nice and close, feel safe and not have to row what seems like halfway to America to get ashore. The extra shelter, of course, means that the water is flatter and you have a quieter night, free of the dreaded rolling, or so I assumed until this August.

Late summer of 2009 saw some exceptionally big tides. These were of a magnitude that would have any sensible fisherman steering straight for the pub, but I and the rest of the 'plaisanciers', buoyed up by the confidence that comes with a decent diesel engine, kept right on yachting. We'd had a rare calm spell and I decided to spend a night or two in Sark, where anchoring is the only option for the casual caller. I used the might of the big streams to blast me up there in light airs from Brittany and arrived two hours before sunset. I'd opted for one of the bays on the East side of the island because the weather man was muttering about westerly breezes kicking in and a swell from that direction was starting to make itself felt. Anticipating a still night, I swung into my chosen roadstead. Half a dozen craft were there already, which was no problem, but they were all rolling fit to throw their sticks out. Puzzled, I aborted my scheme, started the engine and headed off across the gathering might of the north-going torrent up to Diélette. The tide made mincemeat of the 20 or so miles and I was safely over the sill before dark.

The question was, why was it so rough, but I'd already found the answer a mile outside the Sark anchorages. Passing a shoal with loads of water over it, the boat suddenly began leaping about like a duck in a fairground shooting gallery. As the huge tide rattled over the uneven bottom, it was cutting up the otherwise glassy water into a fair copy of the view through the window of my washing machine. Spring tides again. Vives-eaux. Ignore them at your peril. The devil's in them. The reason for my lifetime of gentle neap-tide nights wasn't because I was close in after all. It was just that the slack streams hadn't disturbed the sleeping giant.

The following morning I came across an unexpected manifestation of the old enemy. I paid the charming harbour mistress four Euros to access their WiFi for my on-board Internet connection. It worked first go. I managed my emails and slid off for a spot of lunch, returning at low water with the tide well down despite the protecting sill. After a snooze, I tried to go on-line again for the latest weather and, guess what? Not a peep could I get until the rising tide had levitated me from my private black hole of zero reception.

The old fishermen never thought of that one. I did the only thing I could. I clapped on my best hat, shut the hatch and headed straight for the Bar du Port.

STRIKE A LIGHT

An escape from almost certain tragedy shows that flares will never go out of fashion

Looking back to when I first sailed away in 1970, I sometimes think my memory must be playing me up. In today's world of EPIRBS, liferafts and the general atmosphere of safety at any price, it's hard to credit the minimalist approach aboard the good ship *Johanne*. We were outward bound from the Hamble towards Madeira and it was February. I'd like to report that all had gone well until one night in mid-Biscay, but I'm afraid I can't. The boat was a shapely 90-ton wooden trading ketch recently retired from the Baltic. At 70 feet on deck, she flaunted a jaunty sheer that swept low amidships before rising fore and aft to promise dry feet to the helm and a fighting chance to any adventurer on the focsle head.

Progress wasn't impressive on the night in question, partly because we'd broken the bowsprit in the series of gales that had clobbered us since clearing the Lizard, and partly because it was blowing old boots yet again. The mate and I had the middle watch and we were hove to. The BBC were offering, 'Southwesterly Storm 10 continuing,' The waves had reached prodigious proportions, although luckily for morale it was too dark to size them up. A recent sortie forward had revealed that our oil navigation lamps had blown out via the vents designed to baffle the wind while admitting oxygen for combustion. Nowadays, such heavy copper units are reserved for pub walls. Ours were mounted in traditional lamp screens seized to the shrouds at shoulder height. Neither of us fancied clambering up and, as my superior observed, they'd be snuffed again in no time, so we hunkered down into our pilot coats and did our best to look out.

Seeing anything in those conditions was a hit-and-miss affair, and squinting into the gale was so painful that we were half-blind in that direction. Suddenly, around 0200, two white lights appeared high up in the eye of the wind. Steamer masthead lights, for certain. We could tell they were close, because they were pitching and writhing slowly in the waves. They were also squarely in line and our boat was dead in the water. Seconds later, we smelt her oil smoke as she rose on a big one and showed us her side lights. Red and green, and too far apart to offer a crumb of comfort. We were about to be run down, very soon indeed.

With our insides turning to water, we considered calling the hands to try and get under way, but it was going to be far too late. If the ship cut us in two, all our bright futures would condense into another statistic: 'presumed lost with all hands'. We hadn't a liferaft and would stand no chance whatever. Then the mate reached a decision. Squirming down the companionway to the master's accommodation, he handed up the white handheld flare someone with foresight had clipped to the bottom of the ladder. We'd read the instructions in fairer weather so we knew how to fire it in the dark. I grabbed it and waded forward past the battened-down cargo hatch. Despite being half under water, I had never made the journey to the focsle head so smartly. Steadying myself on the splintered remains of the bowsprit, I struck the detachable bottom of my flare against the top. No auto-fire mechanisms in those days! The flare sputtered for an agonising second, then burst into more light than I'd have believed possible.

I'd already decided not to look at it, but even staring away from the flame, the sight was apocalyptic. The towering mass of the backed staysail was illuminated for its whole height. So was the deep-reefed main, as well as a massive swell rolling away with foam down its back.

Right aft I could see the mate hollering down the hatch for the crew to come up on deck and save themselves. Turning to weather, I confronted our certain doom. Then, just when all seemed lost, the ship's green light faltered and went out, the steaming lights separated and the red swept by glowing like a coal from hell breathed on by the Devil himself. The ship passed so close I could see the rust on her plating.

The flare faded just as the stern lamp appeared. I chucked it over the side and tottered back aft like a zombie. The cook was up. Without a word she handed us the whisky bottle. I've never been more grateful for a dram.

I've been thinking about this incident in the light of some recent high-tech suggestions about how we can avoid being hit by ships. These include strobes which could cause chaos in narrow seas if enough of us used them. Special yacht radar transponders have been mooted, radio calls, active AIS for yachts and heaven knows what else. Well, here's another good idea:

Keep a conscientious lookout, no matter what the weather, be ready to take evasive action before it's too late, and always maintain an in-date white flare handy to the helm for that rare occasion when all else fails. Unless the watch on the bridge is dead or fast asleep he won't miss that – even if he's wearing sunglasses!

RUSSIAN AWAY FROM
FREEDOM

Proposals to restrict sailors' rights to cast off to foreign shores begs the question as to whether this is the thin end of the wedge

I n 1989 I sailed into what was then the communist Russian port of Leningrad. Few western yachts enjoyed this opportunity and my time with the Central Yacht Club of Trade Unions proved a salutary experience. The members were as bemused by our circumstances as we were by theirs. Their yachts were all state-owned, which meant that so long as you kept your nose clean and finally made skipper, you were master or mistress under God without having to pay up. Unfortunately, there was a rather serious catch.

If you wanted a day out with your chums, or even take a quick sail after work, you were obliged to obtain clearance from the authorities, deliver a crew list, state where you were going and when you expected to be back, then report when you did return – and you weren't allowed more than seven miles from base. Arriving 1500 miles from home, in our own time, in our own yacht, such draconian restrictions were hard for us to comprehend, especially as the comrades at the club were highly civilised people, more widely read than most westerners, with an appreciation of the arts and sciences that would have left many a UK undergraduate gasping in the weeds. The situation we found in the Soviet Union demonstrated forcibly that the freedoms we had hitherto taken for granted were, in fact, privileges secured by Magna Carta and the Common Law.

One of the joys of EU membership has been the relaxing of interstate borders. The protocol on Customs and Immigration on much of The Continent means that we can drive or sail from one country to another without formalities. You may therefore have wondered why we have to take our passports on a flight to Paris. The answer is that the UK never signed up for unrestricted passage through immigration. That's why we sailors have to pop our passports in with the ship's papers if we're bound for Ireland, France or the Low Countries.

Over the years since the EU arrived, Customs and Immigration have wisely acknowledged that checking every boat in and out as though they were coming from outside the Union is a time-wasting nuisance for all concerned. In the overwhelming majority of cases, they recognise that we pose no threat to national security and leave us alone. The authorities do, however, retain the right to board and search on a random basis if they see fit. So long as they do this in a sensitive way, few of us object. Most actually applaud the strategy which, helps to deter undesirables from trying their hands at yachting in favour of the comparative luxury of hanging off the underside of a truck in the Tunnel.

What grim news it is, therefore, that when the opportunity arises for technology to secure our borders electronically, those charged with doing so are talking recklessly about our having to report each and every trip outside territorial waters. The RYA are engaged in conversations with the 'e-borders team' to try and make them understand that cruising sailors may not know where they will end up, that we may change our crews at the last minute, that press of weather may alter a passage plan totally in mid-stream, and that many of us will simply not be able to file an internet form with ship's papers and full passport details of all hands from the yacht on arrival or departure. I needn't go any further about the obvious practical nonsense inherent in such a scheme. What is infinitely more important is the issue it raises about our freedom of movement, especially as the onus will lie firmly on unwittingly non-compliant sailors to prove their innocence.

At a recent seminar organised by the Northwest RYA, a show of hands was called for as to whether, in principle, we should secure our borders. Very few disagreed. We live in times where the potential for electronics to ease our administrative burden is substantial. No sensible citizen I've met really objects to filling in and delivering a customs form for voyages beyond the EU. The irritation of being obliged to follow this procedure for the Channel Islands is one I don't propose to examine here. If we could clear in and out for America electronically I've no doubt it would be handy. It will happen sooner or later anyway. So far, so good. When it comes to the EU, however, matters are very different. Not everyone agrees that membership has been an unmitigated benefit for the British, but one unexpected bonus has been how the human face of Customs and Immigration has wisely not pressed its rights to stamp every passport each time we pop across to France or Dublin in our yachts. This choice has made us feel more inclined to assist them in their efforts to keep our borders tight, and I defy any bureaucrat to produce evidence of illegal immigrants and terrorists in large numbers sneaking into Blighty on private yachts. Besides, just as we pay our road taxes and speeding fines to subsidise joyriders never followed up by the 'safety teams' operating the cameras, those who wish us ill via small craft will no doubt fail to file their e-forms. Mostly, they will get away with it.

Applying e-borders to private yachts plying their lawful occasions within EU waters is logistically impractical and constitutionally un-acceptable. It is simply too close for comfort to the old Trade Union Yacht Club in Leningrad, and it would take only a small step to ratchet up the control level to have us report every day sail on pain of criminal conviction. Unlike the soviet Russians, we can still write to our MPs and lobby the RYA to redouble their efforts to keep this thing within reasonable and workable proportions. Failure to do so may well see us sleep-walking into slavery.

ALL SUGGESTIONS
WELCOME

Never ignore inexperienced crew – they may just have the answer to your prayers

Ah, take one consideration with another,
A policeman's lot is not a happy one!

So complained the sergeant of the Boys in Blue when called upon to tackle the Pirates of Penzance. The average cruising instructor might well say the same. My own life certainly wasn't filled with joy when excessive zeal left me moored by the propeller in mid-Solent one sunny Bank Holiday weekend.

Despite the busy waters my course was going swimmingly, except that there wasn't a buoy to be had anywhere for mooring practice. I did find one or two in the Beaulieu River, but they were short of elbow room and the neighbouring yachts looked expensive. I was getting desperate until, cruising west with a Force 4 easterly and three knots of following tide, I hit on what I naively imagined to be a smart idea. I would lay my kedge in open water, buoy the end of the warp and throw it over the side. Instant mooring; problem solved!

We kedged successfully in around thirty feet; the sea was flat, offering a perfect wind-with-tide pickup opportunity. With that sort of tide, my favourite technique is to approach on a close reach, playing the mainsheet as required while keeping the buoy steady against some background feature. The judgement call arrives when the student is nearly there, because he must then spill wind to lose way and let the transit begin to open. At the last moment, the boat luffs into the stream shedding what's left of her way as the foredeck crew pick up the mooring.

The first three students stopped creditably close to my fender, then Bert took the tiller. We'd been coming in on alternate tacks to avoid re-ducing the exercise to a rote, and Bert selected a distant but conspicuous Guernsey cow as his bench mark. She proved an unlucky choice. He'd had the whole herd to pick from and all her mess-mates were enjoy-ing a nice siesta. Unfortunately, Buttercup decided to take a sprightly trot down-tide just as Bert was distracted by a fouled mainsheet. This wretched juxtaposition left him wandering upstream of his objective and, as he bore away towards the makeshift buoy, it was obvious the boat wasn't going to stop.

Bert might have blown his tactical position, but there was nothing wrong with his aim. As he shoved the helm down for the *coup de gras*, the yacht ran over the buoy like a truck over a hedgehog; then her bow fell away from the wind and off we went downtide.

'Have you got it?' he asked optimistically.

'Not a hope, mate. Too fast. It's underneath us somewhere.'

'Better go round again then,' said Bert, ever the optimist, but we didn't. Instead, we were brought up short with a horrible twang as our 'P' bracket snagged the bight of the kedge warp and my best polyform jammed itself into the prop. There we sat with the main pulling bravely, the tide ripping under our stern, and me feeling like the biggest idiot in the West as happy holidaymakers cruised by on both sides.

My first priority was to lash the helm amidships, roll the genoa and wrestle down the mainsail, but one of the lads had read his Day Skipper book and sensibly suggested that we hoist the anchor ball to avoid being run down. With all these accomplished we were legal and comparatively safe, so long as the shaft wasn't dragged out of the stern tube. I couldn't face the idea of sinking and the tide wasn't going to slacken much for four hours, so waiting for slack water was hardly an option. Clearly, we must grab the warp somehow and relieve the load so we could heave in the anchor, but achieving this proved far from simple. Motoring astern would clearly have been suicidal. Grappling the warp with the boathook was easy, but the boat had no sugar-scoop stern and the load was so great that lifting the warp near enough to the surface to get a hand on it proved a non-starter. The angle was awkward and we just hadn't the muscle. My mind was blank, so I threw the issue open to all hands, hoping for some lateral thinking.

'Why not launch the dinghy?' said Bert, anxious to redeem himself.

I could have hugged him. We pumped it up and bunged it over in short order. With the two strongest guys hooking up the bight of the kedge warp close enough to the surface for me to get hold of it, I was able to lie in the dink and bend a spare sheet to it with a rolling hitch. We led this inboard to a primary cockpit winch and the crew cranked a few feet of the kedge warp aboard as easily as kiss my hand. The buoy remained firmly wrapped in the prop, but we now had a slack bight of the warp in the cockpit. We stoppered this off and transferred the slack to the other winch; then we wound in the anchor and trundled home under canvas.

As we sailed alongside in Cowes, I reflected on how it can pay to listen to everyone in a crisis, even a first-voyager. I also made a mental note to teach Day Skippers how to tie a rolling hitch under water.

SPIRITS OF THE SEA

Do historic vessels benefit from mysterious helping hands left behind by original owners who never really signed off?

D o you believe in ghosts? Based on the evidence below, I do. I used to own a pilot cutter that worked before the First World War when people went to church on Sundays. She'd never been restored since Pilot Morrice of Barry sold her in 1922 after a decade spent roaming the Bristol Channel under sail seeking ships to buy his services. Morrice was long dead by the time I took his cutter back to Barry, South Wales in 1982. It was a quiet night full of fog. The boat was still running under her original oil navigation lamps as we drifted up on the flood, guided by DR, leadline and 'trust-in-the-Lord'. I was half-asleep on my watch below when I heard the ancient cry, 'Where bound, Captain?'

There followed a muffled exchange before the response rang out, loud and clear.

'We are the Barry pilot!' Then footfalls, followed by silence.

91

Of course, as day broke I convinced myself I'd been dreaming, but my spinal cord had crawled out of my backbone at 0300.

I thought no more of this until a year later when the elderly cutter was hove-to 100 miles off the coast of Greenland. The gale was well within her comfort zone, but we had two problems. Because it was howling straight off the ice, it was brutally cold, and the wind had risen so rapidly from Force 5 that we'd fantasised things would get better just as quickly. The boat had no winches and, not fancying the muscle-cracking reef purchases, we'd optimistically failed to heave down all our reefs while we still could. Now it was blowing Force 9 with hailstones cutting our cheeks. The solid pine mast was whipping like a fly rod, the soaking flax mainsail weighed a good 400lb and the boom was a 30ft pitch-pine spar tipping the scales at five hundredweight. The whole shooting match was topped off with a solid 25ft gaff. Too late, we fell to the tackles, but even five young men hadn't the strength to clap in those tucks. Our only hope of saving the rig was to drop the sail altogether.

We were lying-to close-hauled with the jib stowed, the staysail aback and the wheel lashed to weather. Somehow we had to persuade her to luff up so we could dump that 800 sq ft of canvas onto the deck rather than into the North Atlantic. The master plan was to let draw the staysail so she could gather way. The lashed helm would swing her into the wind and we'd throw off the main halyards. The weight aloft would ensure it all tumbled down.

The crucial issue was going to be grabbing the gaff, so I stationed myself aft with a length of heavy three-strand to secure the end. The rest we'd play by ear. We waited for a 'smooth' in the seas, then eased the staysail across and watched the classy old girl whoosh up to the wind.

'Leggo!' yelled the mate, and half-a-tennis-court's worth of mainsail flogged down on top of us. Then the staysail blew the bow off the wind, leaving us beam-on to the tempest. The guys dived for cover behind the hatches as the canvas went mad. I tried to grapple the gaff by heaving in on the leech of the sail, but the boltrope ripped my fingernails out. The sail was doing serious damage all round and I hadn't the faintest clue what to do next when suddenly the gaff flipped inboard and sat patiently on top of the shoulder-high boom. As I stared in disbelief at this physical impossibility, I swear I heard a stern Welsh voice.

'I can't hold it for ever, lad. Are you just goin' to stare at it, or will you take a turn and save yourself?'

With frozen hands I whipped the tie around that dreadful spar while the crew somehow lashed up the thrashing flax. Then we all staggered below to the bogey stove where I pondered profoundly on things visible and invisible.

Six years later, Pilot Morrice made his final appearance when the boat was left rafted on piles with the vintage French pilot boat *Jolie Brise*. The morning after the 1987 'hurricane', I drove down to check them out, only to find the harbour master towing the pair of them back upriver. Together they made around 85 tons.

'What happened?' I asked as he tossed me a line.

'They broke away,' he said, 'but somebody let go your main anchor. Snug as a pair of ducks, they were. . .'

The cutter's antique windlass was so eccentric that no stranger would have stood a chance of working it. In any case, why would anyone clamber onto a pair of ancient craft on such a night, perform impossible heroics, then disappear. Not human nature, is it? It was the pilot again. Who else?

I've known other boats with guardian angels. Not all of them have had so obvious a connection, and not every boat has been as historic as mine was. When and why do they come aboard? Sometimes as I sail today's sparkling seas, I wonder what happened to Pilot Morrice. His boat's long gone for rebuild and there's so little of the original left that he's probably jumped ship. I certainly haven't met up with him recently, so I can only hope he hasn't forgotten the lads and lassies who sailed his cutter so far with such dreams in their hearts. However sophisticated we become, we never know when we'll need a helping hand.

SKIPPING WITH JOY

Recycle an old bit of kit and you'll put a smile on your face while you save the planet

I'm a great believer in the seamanlike practice of recycling. Old cans of paint which, like yesterday's rice pudding, only need the skin lifting, bolts trodden into the dust, half-used rolls of tape, you just don't know what you're going to need offshore. A locker-full of unlikely oddments can downgrade a crisis into a repair.

Ashore, the traditional source of this sort of bounty was the skip. For some reason, however, an encouragingly fruitful trend during the Thatcher era seems to have been reversed by the current administration. I don't recall anything in the Queen's speeches about a crackdown on mariners throwing stuff away, yet things have undoubtedly gone to the dogs. Twenty years ago I lived aboard on the South Coast. The mid-winter neighbours included a young couple on a tiny classic and a Kiwi subsisting in a rotting Volvo hidden round the back of the car park. So fertile a source was the skip that we called it 'the chandlery'.

'Morning, Charlie,' I'd greet the sailor. 'Anything in the shop today?'

'Nothing for me, Mate. Nice old block under that coil of wire though. Two sheaves and a becket. Just wants a clean-off. Ideal for your boat.'

And so it continued, especially after the weekend when the plunder ran layers deep. One Sunday evening I scored an echo sounder, a forty-fathom hank of 18mm three-strand, a bottle of Gordon's gin with plenty left and a folio of Spanish charts. The rope looked a bit ratty but had loads of life in it. I still keep it in my focsle and it enjoyed a night of glory only recently when it relieved a shaky pontoon cleat by securing my bow to a distant wall. The charts were black-and-white, but none the worse for that. Although I navigate with a plotter now, they still do their job because the rocks are pretty permanent and the almanac can update the lights if necessary. Those charts remain unbeatable value as backup when I'm down that way. The sounder served me well for many a season, and the gin gave equal satisfaction, if somewhat shorter-lived.

Although the salad days of the dumpster are over, I still take a peek on Sunday evening before I toddle back to the homestead. Sometimes there are chunks of hardwood for my boat stove, and I did find a handsome mahogany cabinet complete with glass shelves last autumn, but generally the thing's full of rubbish. The sea is not so impoverished. I once met a lady fisherman in Finland who remained optimistic despite the inhospitable nature of her surroundings and the terrible toll pillaged from her livelihood by Russian vacuum ships.

'What's left for you to net?' I asked her as she set out one grey evening.

'Ah,' she replied with a merry grin, 'You never know what you find swimming in the sea!'

And so it has proved for me. As the skip harvest has declined, my catch in open water has multiplied. I haven't bought a fender in ages. They're out there after every gale, cruising up and down with the tide waiting to be grabbed. The fresh ones are best – no barnacles – and every now and again one shows up that's the right size. A different sort of find was an orthopedic pillow which I came across 100 miles off Nova Scotia. As we lugged it aboard I hoped that when wrung well out it might cure my mate of his snoring, but in this it was a failure. I kept it all the same, and its time came shortly afterwards when a problem with the stern gland obliged me to crawl across the engine to apply the ritual spanner. The Lister was red-hot, knobbly and space between it and the deckhead was only six inches thicker than my waistline. A nasty prospect, until I remembered the pillow. Slipped between me and the action, it provided both comfort and insulation.

The most recent addition to my equipment was spotted by my wife when homeward bound from France. I've never liked radar reflectors much because, although they do an important job, the older-style ones have ruined the look of many a pretty rig and they generate needless windage. I really fancied one of those clever new ones that are so slender you hardly notice them, but cash isn't endless and one must prioritise. Imagine my delight when she pointed out a mint example bobbing by. Keeping it in view in Force 5 while I executed my best man-overboard pickup in a long while was a trial, but she grabbed it at the first pass and hoisted it in triumph. I sold the original on eBay and am now the thoroughly modern sailor.

Some years back, an elderly North Atlantic islander who was emptying a large bag of garbage over his local harbour wall remarked to me that, 'the sea will take it away.'

He'd know, wouldn't he? What he didn't mention was that, given time and patience, what goes in will also come back, but maybe not exactly to where it started.

THE ABILITY FOR STABILITY

A drinks party on board creates a distinct feeling of instability

'Excuse me', I said to the gent in the blazer and club tie. 'Do you mind if I stand outboard of you.' He shuffled aside.

We were part of a crush on the deck of an ancient sailing pilot cutter I used to own. It was a yacht club meet, she was rafted up to the commodore's yacht and I had edged over to our well-fendered toe rails. Wine was flowing, chums were waving across the press of bodies and the evening sun lit the lower reaches of the Beaulieu River to the buzz of happy voices. There was only one problem. Having just sailed the boat 10,000 miles or so in all weathers, mostly bad, I knew her intimately, and the way she felt right now was not encouraging.

In short, she was crank – an old-fashioned term for 'marginally unstable' which I prefer to its more scientific successor. When you board a boat that's crank, there's something about the way she lurches that turns you sick. This was a hefty vessel, 50ft on deck, 45ft on the waterline, displacing well over 30 tons. How many bodies she might safely carry had never crossed my mind, but when I felt her swooping under my feet that evening my first reaction was to shunt over to where I could hop off.

A quick head count showed 80 people on deck.

'Say 12 stone each,' I mused. 'That's $1\frac{1}{2}$ hundredweight – about 14 humans to the ton. . .'

The flesh count totted up to six tons, a shocking insult to the boat's ballasting arrangements, especially since the iron was all in the bilge with none on the keel. There was plenty of it, but the festivities were playing 'Old Harry' with the centre of gravity.

Just then, I caught sight of my wife jumping around on the main hatch, beckoning me fiercely to come below. I elbowed my way down the companion ladder to be met by that running water sound no skipper wants to hear.

'It's the loos,' she whispered. 'They're both overflowing.'

The extra weight had depressed the boat so far below her marks that my Baby Blakes were siphoning Lord Montagu's river merrily into the bilge. I could only speculate about the huge volume of water it took to fill that cavern, but the first job was to shut the seacocks and pin up a sign warning any hopefuls steering for the heads that disappointment awaited them.

You'd think pumping out would be the next step, or maybe advising the revellers to evacuate while they still could, but neither option was attractive. The bilge was cleared by a traditional set-up with a three-inch pipe running down through the deck and a wrought-iron 'village pump' at the top. It needed a bucket of seawater to prime it and the results of its labours spewed all over the planking. The contents of the bilge were far from salubrious, so the prospect of ditching a hundred gallons around the hon. sec's best deck shoes held few charms. I didn't want to confess that my boat was full of water either, because I was inordinately proud of her and she normally never leaked a drop in harbour. I sat tight therefore, and noted with relief that although her roll was noticeably slower at the end, she came back positively enough to convince me she wasn't about to go over.

The crowd finally dispersed with the last of the daylight. Once it was good and dark, the silence of the river was broken only by curlews complaining about the steady clanking of my pump.

I mention this incident from the dank lockers of my past because I have been working on the question of stability this week for the RYA *Manual of Seamanship*. Most of us nowadays know all about GZ curves. For those who don't, these are graphs showing, amongst other things, the angle of heel at which a boat no longer self-rights. Yachts today are coded by various authorities to tell us how safe they may be in awesome weather offshore. The deductions tend to draw heavily on a boat's GZ curve for data, but it gets clearer every year that this graph and the rest of the empirical information are only a part of the story.

I was once obliged to code the pilot boat for a TV series. At great expense I was awarded a bound booklet that told me when to reef her, based on wind speed and heel angle. She had never boasted an anemometer, but the powers that be were satisfied when I produced one of those Christmas cracker blow-in-the-bag devices that purport to measure the wind force, plus a brass pub-wall inclinometer from a car boot sale. It was to the inspector's credit that he had the wisdom to see beyond his clipboard. The boat's inside ballast gave her an indifferent GZ curve, yet she and I weathered many an ocean gale and toughed out one named hurricane. A century ago, when such craft worked winter and summer out in the western approaches to the British Isles, almost none foundered at sea. She was far and away the most seaworthy vessel of her size I have ever encountered.

At the other end of the scale, I have experienced yachts claiming 'category wonderful' seaworthiness which my gut reaction leaves me reluctant to sail beyond the Needles in a moderate gale. Sometimes we do better to trust our instincts than hang our hats on a sheet of mathematics.

SHEER DELIGHT

An inch or two is all that may be needed to transform the everyday into the exceptionally beautiful

Ask anyone around today's waterfronts for the names of some historic designers and I'll bet my dictionary to a bus ticket that the first to be flagged up will include William Fife, G L Watson of George V's *Britannia*, and Charles E Nicholson. The association of these giants with the great yachts of the golden age before WWII made them famous beyond the tiny circle of privilege who paid for their commissions. They were also table talk in humble households who could never hope to tread the decks, yet who willed His Majesty to win as they watched the racing from seaweed-popping rocks and wind-swept piers.

In reality, such big-name draughtsmen and their world would have had little to do with most of us. The designers that *YM* readers might have looked to in those days were a different breed. Some were amateurs and, in a generation where excellence and self-control were taken for granted, they were none the worse for that. My personal favourite is an eye surgeon called Harrison Butler. Running him close for sweetness of line and balance of helm came Linton Hope, Warington Smythe, Norman Dallimore and Albert Strange. I don't know why we never hear mellifluous names like these any more, but if the Prime Minister really wants to discover the essence of Britishness, he might take the time to consider such men. Their stories may have varied, but these artists in the discipline of drawing board and slide rule had one thing in common. They knew how to make a small yacht beautiful.

To lift so potentially humdrum an artefact to the level of high art takes education, study and years of application. Maintaining their standards on the water is the duty of every sailor, even if our boats are brand new and have no more sheer than this morning's paper. Given a halfway decent shape, a yacht's excellence is established by the sum of a thousand details, which is where the rest of us come in.

Take boot-topping, for example – that line painted fore-and-aft just above the waterline to divide antifoul from topside colour. Harrison Butler made a point of picking out this vital boundary on his plans, and it is never parallel sided. The upper edge describes a shallow parabola whose arc lies partway between the flat, lower waterline edge and the sweeping sheerline of the deck. The difference between his curving boot-top and the ruler-straight equivalent often seen today is little more than an inch, yet it brings the yacht to life. Like Mother Nature, the classically styled boat hates a straight line. Many modern cruisers, on the other hand, have a flat sheer. This leaves the designer little option but to mirror it, but if she has even the hint of curve in her deck-line, a touch of movement in the boot-top can work miracles.

The same goes for painted 'sheer strakes', those bands of colour along some hulls that cheat the eye and make them appear lower-slung than they actually are. In the days before fibreglass construction, one plank would be picked out for just the same reason. So why did the wooden boat look so much better? The answer is that a hull plank tapers naturally towards its ends, generally from its lower edge. The paint line was defined by this taper and, however slight it was, it drew the eye upwards to follow the sheer. The shape of the whole boat was enhanced. A parallel line can do the opposite, flattening the sheer and killing any curvature the deck may have stone dead. A cove line whose aft end dips down is disastrous for the same reason, yet more than one well-known manufacturer foists this horror on new owners today.

Another area of forgotten subtleties is the rig. Except in certain specific cases, traditional sail plans with two or more masts went to some pains to keep the spars parallel when viewed beam-on. A ketch or a schooner with her masts sagging outwards at the top looks, not to put too fine a point on it, like a half-split log. Yet every day we see two-masters suffering this gross indignity. It shouldn't take much to put it right, and the yacht will positively sing her gratitude.

Boom angle does a lot for a boat's appearance too. Older-style rigs favoured mainsails cut with the boom well down at the gooseneck, sweeping upwards to the clew. This followed the sheer and, in the days of low freeboard, it kept the sail from rolling into the water downwind. Check any pilot cutter, or one of those American masterpieces like *Ticonderoga* and notice how today's Open 60s have reverted to type. If ever you see such a yacht with her main boom sagging like a door with the top hinge off, find her sailmaker and insist he stops humiliating so fine a vessel. Modern cruisers with flat sheers and high freeboard have no choice but to rig the boom parallel with the water, but many could at least be lowered to a more natural height. The occasional bash on the head for the unwary would be a small price to pay for improving the general view, lowering the centre of effort and allowing the sail to be stowed without a garden ladder.

Let's end with the spreaders. When the Almighty invented these, he intended them to bisect the angle the cap shroud makes at their outboard end. This slight upward 'kick' delivers maximum efficiency. It also lifts the whole boat visually like a bird flexing her wings. Stuff them square across the mast, and the spar somehow loses both height and grace. An inch or two is often enough. On G L Watson's mighty *Britannia* you might be looking at a whole foot, but Harrison Butler and Linton Hope weren't designing for kings.

THE BIG BANG

In 2006, the wisdom of banning maroons to summon lifeboat crews was called into question

'Boom!' goes the first maroon. Doors open, and anyone out on the waterfront looks skywards for a second flash. 'Boom!' the next explosion blasts out far overhead and the whole town knows it's a shout for the lifeboat.

Today, the maroon's official job is to back up the pagers which all crew carry, yet it achieves far more than this. It broadcasts what's happening to anyone who isn't stone deaf, it advises boats in the harbour to move out of the way, and it slips the wink to the guys in the Mission to Seamen so they can put the soup on. Harbourmasters need to be in the loop so as to keep the channel clear for the safety of the boat and those in her path, ferry operators may prefer to stand off, bridge operators can help control traffic in certain ports, and so on. The maroons are also a priceless reassurance to any casualties close enough inshore to hear and see, while the wild abandon of their call followed by the crew running down to the harbour and the big boat growling seawards on a filthy night stirs the soul of anyone not dead from the heart outwards.

I for one am far more likely to shove a wedge of folding money into the collecting box after an experience like that.

Although lifeboat maroons have been part of our coastal culture since 1826, the RNLI have now decided to reduce their use with the ultimate aim of phasing them out. The reason is. . . . Yes, you've guessed it! It's good old 'Health and Safety'. Concerns have been expressed that the folk of coastal communities are at risk from falling debris from the rockets, which suggests something of a loss of perspective. Compared with the weight of ordnance we shoot into the heavens on bonfire night, the odd lifeboat maroon is small beans, but there isn't much public support for a ban on fireworks. Far more serious is the spectre of a maroon going berserk as it is activated, endangering either the operator or someone else. Recent examples of the latter include a couple of genuine narrow escapes, but further research shows that maroon incidents have historically affected those doing the firing rather than innocents strolling on the promenade.

May 1876 saw coxswain Thomas Williams injured as the maroon was ignited for the brand-new ten-oared Aberystwyth lifeboat. Coxswain Williams went to sea in spite of serious powder burns and successfully recovered a fishing boat with three men which had been missing for 24 hours. In Poole, Miss Daisy Harmar was about to launch the boat that carried her name in 1897 when someone accidentally let off the maroon. The Mayor curtailed his speech earlier than he'd intended, the launchers knocked out the pin holding the boat at the top of the slip, and away she went. No harm was done and the *Harmar* went on to save 60 lives in a successful career spanning almost 30 years. In 1927, however, the coxswain of the Port St Mary boat lost his life firing a maroon to open the local flag day. Last year, a maroon misfired horizontally to fizzle out alongside a café, instead of soaring up to 1100ft where it properly belonged.

Undoubtedly, there is danger from maroons. The present directive is that stations should use them only when specifically appropriate, and the Institute is anxious not to have this option shut down by the Health and Safety Executive if a tragedy should ever occur. Maroons are therefore discouraged, but the alternatives are unattractive.

Like the maroon, the pager is a one-way form of communication. Once he's hit the button, the coxswain can only wait to see who will show, but he has no idea of whether it has worked or not, or if all hands have theirs within earshot. When the maroon explodes high overhead, he knows nobody will have missed it unless they have *EastEnders* turned up so loud that Dirty Den is rattling the telly, or they're out of town.

Noise certainly does the trick, and one proposal under consideration is to substitute a siren of serious proportions. This sounds sensible enough, except that those curmudgeons who currently complain at being woken in the small hours by a bang that's saving some poor sailor in trouble will enjoy the prolonged howling even less. I suspect that the racket will end up driving the rest of us crazy and have exactly the opposite social effect of the much-loved pyrotechnics.

Most important of all, the fear that the Institution might one day be sued by someone injured by a maroon could well be more than offset by loss of donations associated with the downgrading of the lifeboat to a silent service. No shortage of unpaid crew volunteers blights my local station, yet their equally brave brothers in the fire service struggle to make up numbers despite being paid a retainer. There is something inherently charismatic about the blue boats and their crews. The explosion of the maroons as the gale rattles the church windows is its manifestation. Maybe one life will be saved some day by removing them from service, but the boats are saving lives all the time. In the final reckoning, more may be lost if the maroons are banned.

A WISE INVESTMENT?

Should we be protecting our maritime past or investing in the youth of tomorrow?

D id you know that the projected bill for re-establishing the *Cutty Sark* as a tourist attraction stands at £34,000,000? Over £20,000,000 of this is public funding. As the only surviving tea clipper, the ship is clearly of national importance. It's unfortunate that she has recently been severely damaged by fire, because little of what a future visitor may see will be the actual vessel which raced home from China. The situation raises a sea of issues.

Rather than the extensive restoration planned, a second body of informed opinion holds that *Cutty Sark* would be better conserved as she is. A third group would have her broken up, or 'deconstructed', under rigorous guidelines so that lessons will not be lost. On the face of it, you pay your money (many of us will), and you take your choice. The reality is not so simple.

Since this column was written, the *City of Adelaide* question has been satisfactorily resolved and the bill for _*Cutty Sark* has escalated to over £40 million.

106

A WISE INVESTMENT?

Up in Scotland, the only other British clipper is quietly subsiding into dust. Lacking metropolitan interest and what Nelson's captains called 'patronage', the emigrant ship *City of Adelaide* which carried many a hopeful colonist to South Australia is comparatively unheard of in the Northern Hemisphere. Permission has been sought to demolish her. Funds are thin, the pressure is on, and only the efforts of our National Historic Ships body stand between her and the knackers. If a choice of restoration were on the cards, it is arguable that more of the *City of Adelaide* remains than her younger sister down in Greenwich.

You might by now be questioning the relevance of expensive antique ships in times as dire as these. If you feel that money on this scale would be better spent on humanity suffering in a straitened world, I for one wouldn't argue. Society needs all the help it can get, so it is with some relief that I report on a fourth accepted way of preserving our maritime inheritance. The step-ladder of heritage options begins at the bottom with deconstruction; next comes conservation, followed by restoration. At the top from the sailor's point of view, blows a breath of fresh, salt air. 'Conserve the original, then send a replica to sea'.

It's been said with some authority that Britain could build an ocean-capable clipper and have change from the cost of *Cutty Sark*. You have to ask whether that might not be better value. Imagine a sharp clipper: her perfectly proportioned rig uncompromised by political correctness, with no extra deck houses and a hold for dry cargo; with a sheer to inspire poets in an age when ships look like apartment blocks, and the red duster whipping out from a tapering spanker gaff. She could come up to London, but she could also show what Britain is really made of in ports far away.

Talk is cheap, however, and such a project must either be externally funded or managed with a touch of genius. In any case, why should anyone outside the seafaring community take the slightest notice? The answer lies with a generation whose needs outstrip those of two ancient ships by an incalculable factor.

Whatever the reason, we all know that our cities and countryside teem with a growing army of dangerously disaffected youth. Many end up in institutions where they cost us the taxpayers about a thousand pounds a week to keep under lock and key. Experience shows that, safely inside, they complete their education at the feet of masters in the school of crime. Once released, they re-offend in large numbers. Their life is set on a path to nowhere at the expense of us all.

The best thing the sea can offer these young people today is a passage on a sail training ship if they are lucky enough to secure a bursary – if indeed they'd want it anyway. There could, however, be a thrilling alternative. Cargoes exist that can be viably transported by long-voyage sailing vessels. Were our clipper ship to carry the world's merchandise to Australia and back via the Southern Ocean and Cape Horn, manned by young offenders mixed with sailing professionals, her crew would quickly learn their own value. Respect for others would follow as the night the day.

Elemental danger, exuberance, humility and self-esteem. These are all well-known to the sailor. They are also fundamentals sadly missing for those who grow up with no father and no community, under the influence of drug-pushers and gang leaders. Such basics of life are self-taught by harsh reality on the upper yards in a gale of wind where there can be no compromise and there is nowhere to hide. The result is simple – pride in being part of a team with a serious, physical job to do.

Given a kick-start from sponsors or public funding, such a ship can be built commercially, but she cannot pay her way from cargo alone. Add the cash largely wasted by locking away young offenders and the books balance. The mathematics of such a project were worked out exhaustively over a decade ago by the Renaissance Trust. They were scrapped because the government of the day feared the backlash if a lad were lost. Of equal concern was a putative press reaction about 'luxury cruises'. For the idea to be reborn, someone high in the Home Office must have the courage to look beyond these side issues and the vision to open the prison door. Given the crew and the funding, the rest would surely follow. Then we could again see proper vessels being built, creating jobs and fresh skills in deprived areas, a new generation of sailors, a green transport system, and hope for the hopeless. All for less than one thousandth of what it cost to bail out Northern Rock.

CENTENARY
CELEBRATIONS

Yachting Monthly's 100-year anniversary flagged up the way a surprising amount had not changed

A few years after *Yachting Monthly's* 50th anniversary I found a battered volume in my local library called *Deep Water and Shoal* that defined my future. It described a circumnavigation in the 1930s by a young American who paid next to nothing for his boat, put to sea on a wing and a prayer, and proceeded to have the sort of adventures that would quicken the blood of any schoolboy. Well before I was 30 I was on my way in a similar craft. Technology had moved ahead a bit by the 1970s. We had electric clocks of a sort to give us our longitude, life rafts were available for those who chose to divert valuable funds in that direction, some people even had radios, but for me at least, not much else had changed.

Now we've arrived at the magazine's centenary, I'm thinking about all this and wondering which period of the last hundred years would be my personal choice for contented cruising. By comparison with earlier voyaging, today's blue water world is almost unrecognisable. There's every possibility for distressed deep-water sailors to be fished out of the drink, dodgy landfalls are a thing of the past and the hungry mariner can even dig in the freezer for a packet of baby peas to go with the mid-ocean Sunday roast. All very tempting, but on balance I'm inclined to believe that if one's motivations for ocean cruising are a youthful search for adventure, comradeship and inner satisfaction, the 1930s were the best of times. If the master-plan is to empty the family bank account to maximise comfort and minimise risk – the twin holy grails of the middle-aged – we're better served by 2006!

I have no immediate plans for returning full-time to the gypsy life of my youth. Like most of us, I now sail when I can and pay my taxes like a gentleman, but my servitude is lightened by reading Maurice Griffiths' accounts of inshore cruising between the two world wars. Not for him the heady world of yacht racing with paid hands doing all the sailing. 'MG' was a Corinthian, a man who handled his own yard work and pulled his own ropes come sunshine, gale or creeping fog. Sounds familiar? You bet it does. That's us isn't it? Sure, our hulls these days are mostly low-maintenance, so we no longer have to hammer in caulking while dried out on the sands between tides, but we still have lines to splice, antifouling to slap on, and job lists that get longer not shorter. However, two transformations have occurred since the days of MG and his chums that flag up his time as my own golden age.

The first is a revolution in society which has nothing directly to do with sailing. The family motor car has clipped our cruising wings just as surely as it has liberated other aspects of our lives. Boats generally had no engines in the 1930s, so a weekend cruise on the East Coast would have been curtailed almost to extinction if sailors had been obliged to return to base to pick up the Volvo estate. Fortunately, some visionary in the LNER dreamed up the 'yachtsman's weekend return'. Most communities had stations in the halcyon days before Dr Beeching fettled up his axe, and this flexible ticket allowed you to ride the train to and from any village to suit your boat's movements. You could travel down to where you'd left her last week, take the tide and wind to a new destination, leave your little yacht bobbing on a spare mooring in the charge of a local boatman, then grab the milk train up to town on Monday morning. No gruesome marina charges were levied, your dinghy was safe, and as often as not the ancient mariner would stock up the boat ready for your return on Friday afternoon with paraffin, tea, a can of bully beef and half-a-dozen eggs from his wife's best chicken. Every weekend became an adventure into the uncertainty of natural forces, a freedom which the car has effectively denied us.

The second change spins off from the first. You could say it's increasing noise, but I prefer to call it the lack of silence – the sort of silence you can feel. One night last winter saw my somewhat 'retro' boat moored up a favourite gunk-hole. The yacht on the next buoy had finally shut down her blown-air heating and the wind had died to a whisper. Out on deck the frost was thickening and Orion strode masterfully across the sky as the Spring flood faded out on top of the tide, but I was warm down below. As I took a sip at my nightcap, a coal slipped down in the bogey stove with a muted clink and I realised that I could actually hear the oil lamp burning on the table. Away across the marshes a curlew piped at the stars and suddenly I knew that MG and all the host who've steered true and entered harbour ahead of us were with me in spirit. Perhaps 2006 isn't such a bad year to go cruising. After all, we can't turn back the clock. We just need to remember how to be still.

UNDER PRESSURE

A secret harbour in a storm during 2007's lousy summer sees blood pressure rising as the mercury plummets

'If things don't get any better, they'll stay the same as they are,' observed a shipmate peering out of the companionway long ago in a mid-Biscay storm. The implication was, of course, that conditions couldn't deteriorate beyond their present nadir. Anyone optimistic enough to go cruising in home waters last summer will probably feel that he couldn't have put it more succinctly himself. Most of us have our own stories of blown-out plans and cabin fever. Mine involved a lengthy sojourn in Brest.

The Rade de Brest is only 20 miles south of the official end of the English Channel. When the going gets tough outside, it's as fine a natural harbour as you'll find. The only problem is the marina. Huge and at the end of nowhere special, it is well-run, convenient and an excellent jumping-off point for airports. However, although I've been glad of these features many times, the sprawling desert of its pontoons grows charmless all too soon. Being forewarned of this, I swept into the Rade past the Napoleonic gun emplacements that once kept Nelson's frigates at bay, and sailed on until the chart ran out a mile or two up the beautiful River Aulne. From here, you're on your own with only Mr Cumberlidge's excellent pilot book for company. Press on regardless, however, and three hours later you arrive, still in deep water, at a lock and a fine modern sluice. Inside the gates lies the Breton canal system. A mile further on, after passing beneath a spectacular stone viaduct, you're alongside the old village waterfront at Port Launay.

This little-known paradise has no harbourmaster, no charges, and no facilities you'd want to use, but it has permanent high water, a clean stone wall with genuine pink daisies growing out of it, a sweet little boulangerie with a friendly baker, a travelling pizza van and a useful town a short dinghy ride further up. The canal is part of the local psyche, having been there for two centuries. It's also my favourite port in a storm. This was a good thing because after being stuffed in there by five days of strong northerlies, I was then neaped for a week before a further craven refusal to face the westerly gales that followed.

The EU recently paid millions of our money to upgrade the sophisticated sluice, only to decide the place would have to be shut down because the 'water quality' was not up to some scratch or other. The lock was to be demolished and the riverside abandoned to an acreage of tidal mud not seen since before the Battle of Trafalgar. There's good news, however. The French don't put up with rubbish from Brussels – at least, the Bretons don't. A massive outcry complete with public meetings and soapbox oratory resulted in this nonsense being scrapped, so I'll be OK next time the weather turns to the bad as I scramble round the corner at Ushant.

Less fortunate, it seems, are the manufacturers of old-fashioned mercury barometers. We on yachts don't use these. The brass one my wife taps while glaring at every passing cloud, is an aneroid. You may even have an upmarket electric one, but the mercury barometer remains the historic fount of all wisdom. If you're not lucky enough to have one on the hall wall, you'll remember them from school physics, literally measuring the column supported by atmospheric pressure – not in some fabricated unit but in millimetres or even real inches. You may recall the fun we used to have when some clown spilled the mercury.

We'd chase the tiny shining spheres of toxic metal – magically molten at room temperature – around the classroom floor, sweeping them up with a dustpan and brush. Even in those sunny days of political incorrectness none of my form-mates was fool enough to take a refreshing draught of the stuff, and most of us are not yet exhibiting symptoms of heavy metal poisoning. Despite this general common sense the EU, abetted by the British government, have banned further production of these lovely and ancient tools. Our leaders offer us this protection while working towards a world where we all will be obliged to use light low-energy bulbs containing. . . . . guess what – Mercury!

'Ah, but the lights only use tiny quantities,' they say. Well, the secretary of the British Barometer Makers Association points out that of the 300 tons used in the EU every year, less than 30 kilos goes into new barometers in the UK. Not much, is it, to justify shutting down a world-class industry established for centuries?

All this is being done in the name of saving the planet. It seems ironic therefore that the best the British government can manage when confronted with the disgusting slaughter of up to a thousand whales in the Southern Ocean by Japan 'for scientific purposes', is a 'high-level diplomatic protest to the Japanese government following consultation with like-minded anti-whaling countries.' The European Commission says it urges Japan to reconsider its decision and stop the hunt. Hardly strong medicine. Australia, on the other hand, has sent a coastguard ship to monitor and film the whole grisly process in the hope of gathering enough data to leave the whalers without a case, while the crew of a Greenpeace ship are putting their bodies in front of the harpoons.

If Britain and the EU are serious about the environment, we need to do more about the real crimes.

TRIALS AND
TRIBULATIONS

Buying a boat is a costly business. The message is clear: don't be swayed by boat-show sparkle!

O
ne brisk Sunday afternoon many years ago I found myself motoring back into the Hamble River at rush-hour at the helm of my first boat, a 22-foot wooden cruiser. My crew was a gentleman who had undertaken to buy her subject to two reasonable conditions: 'survey' and 'trial sail'. The survey was yet to come, but I had no fears on that score. We were currently engaged upon the trial sail, and thus far it had gone well. My engine was a single-cylinder two-stroke from a well-known manufacturer and like every one of its vintage I ever ran across, it had its little ways. Starting was rarely an issue. You simply turned on the petrol, swung the handle and it puttered into life. Occasionally it went berserk and refused to release the crank, leaving the operator with no choice but to kill the fuel and cross his fingers until the unit finally faded out. During the interim, you had two chances: either the handle continued whizzing round at unimaginable

speed, or it let go. If it selected the latter option, it smashed through the deck if your luck was in, or the bottom planking if it wasn't. The old darling's other naughty habit was that for reasons I never fathomed, it would rarely keep turning for more than 30 minutes. It then lay doggo for an hour or two, after which it would fire up as though nothing had happened. In those days of unreliable engines, this didn't seem much of a drawback. The working time-span was enough to buzz upriver to my berth, and at sea it was my custom to sail or wait. It was so many months since the unit had been asked to deliver for any longer that I'd forgotten its unwilling tendencies.

Suddenly, however, real life loomed large and ugly. The breeze had died well outside the buoys and my buyer was anxious to get home to his wife's birthday which he had so far avoided on the lame excuse of buying a yacht. I'd started the motor, and it performed as well as it knew how until it packed in off the Rising Sun at Warsash. This left me with a couple of miles to beat against a northerly wind. No problem. The little boat sailed like a witch anyway, so I hoisted the sails and tacked merrily onwards, using the whole width of the river. Sadly for my enterprise, as I cruised out from the moorings a large power boat whose steady bearing I'd been monitoring decided to ignore me and stand on. Closer inspection of the helmsman revealed him to be wrapped around a blonde in a sailor suit and this project was attracting more of his attention than I was. Understandable, of course, but not helpful. He hit me between my best jeans and my backstay. The mast went over the side in fine style and, to cut a long story short, the buyer returned to the bosom of his family by other means. I only saw him again when he decently handed me a bottle of Grant's 'Stand Fast' whisky to sweeten the bad news that he'd bought a fibreglass bilge keeler instead. I've had a soft spot for the brand ever since.

I mention this incident in light of having just visited the Southampton Boat Show. As usual, new boat sales were reported as brisk. I'm sure we're all delighted to hear that, but there's an aspect of buying a boat at a show that makes me uneasy. I know that some experienced people insist on sampling the goods before committing themselves, but many do not. The thought of buying a yacht without a serious sea trial fills me with gloom.

There's a world of difference between walking around generous accommodation spaces when they're upright and when they're bouncing from wave-top to wave-top at 20 degrees of heel. So many questions vital to an owner's happiness remain unanswered.

Do those tiny fiddles on the galley actually work? Can you realistically pull down your pants in the head? Does that neat little seat halfway across the saloon separating the galley from the sitting area trip the cook over backwards from the uphill side when the yacht takes an awkward lurch? Where do you actually sleep at sea in bad weather? On the sail bags? And so on.

Further critical issues that remain unresolved concern the boat's performance. These could be simple questions such as whether the winches are big enough, but they might be more fundamental. A wide-sterned modern cruiser is *prima facie* at risk of developing unanswerable weather helm when she takes a sudden gust with plenty of rag up. Many such craft avoid this tendency by clever design, yet there are plenty which fail miserably. The only way to find out for sure is to give her some stick on a windy day. I know it's hard to work a busy diary around the weather map, but if I were spending a six-figure sum, I'd only lay down my deposit on the traditional understanding, 'Subject to a trial sail on the day of my choice – and it won't be my wife's birthday.'

TROUBLESOME SEAGULLS

An incident with a classically unreliable outboard helps save a marriage

One of the better features of traditional yachts is that even relatively modest ones can carry a solid dinghy. A hard tender can be rowed, especially if it's wooden. A punt that pulls well doesn't need an outboard, and freedom from care is the proper reward for a little easy work. Today, most of us are stuck with inflatables, which puts a decent outboard firmly on top of everyone's list.

This week, I chartered a yacht, only to be told the dinghy motor was 'extra'. I kicked up a fuss on the grounds that a flubber can't make serious progress under its paddles in more than Force 4, but that it remained critical to the yacht's seaworthiness. Never mind pulling across to the pub from the anchor, I raved, what about laying out a kedge when the main halyard has wrapped itself round the propeller? The agent decently capitulated and we got our Honda, but it gave food for thought about how far things have come since we used to augment our sweeps with British Seagull outboards.

I've had a few of these unlamented units in my time. Sometimes they ran, sometimes they didn't. One friend used his as an anchor when he'd lost his ground tackle and his main engine failed. His yacht was drifting in no wind towards her doom in a pile of coral trash when he hove it over the bow on a long line. It held, and he later observed that it did more good on the seabed than it ever had on the transom of his dinghy, although he did complain that it was never quite the same again.

Seagulls were as noisy as their namesakes on the pier at Brixham. They were also twice as smelly and half as reliable, but they did have two advantages over anything sold since. Their advertising slogan read, 'Perfectly simple, everlastingly Seagull.' They were simple all right, though I'm not so sure about the 'perfect' bit, and if 'indestructible' means 'everlasting', you couldn't argue with that either. My daughter, a shrewd business-woman from birth, once pulled one out of the skip at Beaulieu when she was eight years old. It was seized solid, had no propeller and the petrol tank looked as if it had lost an argument with a steam roller. Notwithstanding these minor drawbacks, she lugged it along to the boat jumble and, as the last stragglers were trudging away in triumph or despair, she flogged it to some poor masher for a fiver.

My own Seagull undoubtedly saved my marriage by breaking down on a cruise to Ireland in the late 1980s. It was a Saturday morning in Baltimore and a long dinghy trip up-river to a pub in Skibbereen was mooted. The lady wife fancied a bus-ride to visit a stately home instead. Coffee and buns were promised to those paying a quid at the gate, but she was outvoted and so, under strong protest, we all set off at 0730 to catch the flood to the fleshpots. The Seagull packed up off a drying creek where we paddled towards a stony beach until running aground 20 yards out. My mate and I were fumbling with the spark plug when an aristocratic sort of cove and what was clearly his 'man' appeared from behind a high hedge. We explained our predicament and, without further ado, the honest retainer was detailed off to carry my wife ashore like St Christopher. I waded behind, but, as my mate was about to follow suit, the top chap announced that my man and his could sort out the mechanics while The Quality – which included me – would stroll up to the house for breakfast. My shipmate gave me a bit of a look, but there was nothing to be done, so we popped off through the trees to what turned out to be the very house my bride had been aching to visit. She got the whole tour for free, a noble Irish breakfast thrown in, and a look at parts of the gardens normally only visited by friends of the family.

'Ah well,' said our host as 1000 struck on the grandfather clock, 'I'd better open up and welcome the tourists.'

The Seagull, meanwhile, had been fettled, so we buzzed on up to town in a haze of blue oil-smoke. It could never have happened with the Honda. Sometimes, I wonder whether progress is really worth the expense.

SKIP IT SKIPPER

The days when the sea was treated as a giant waste disposal unit have gone – but don't presume to chuck all your rubbish in the boatyard skip

'There's the stove, you see,' remarked Davies to Carruthers in Erskine Childers' famous novel, *The Riddle of the Sands*. 'I've chucked the old one overboard.'

That was back in 1903 when a man could heave anything he chose into the briny and nobody would say a word about it. In Davies' defence, there were fewer people then and their waste was far less gruesome than the stuff we throw away today, but it does go to show how attitudes have changed.

A few months ago I wrote about lifting things out of skips. This month, we're stuffing them in. In fact, of course, our current 'green-clean' mind-set has been with us far less than a century. It can't be more than 30 years since *YM* editor Des Sleightholme proposed 'The Great *Yachting Monthly* Teabag Throwing Contest'. In those days we all

121

tipped these over the side, and it was great fun employing the teaspoon as a sort of catapult. Top prizes were awarded for clearing the taffrail from the galley, and I recall one well-soaked PG Tips sachet of mine that fetched up in the harbourmaster's moneybag as he came alongside with his ticket machine. I got no dispensation for my bowsprit that morning.

It didn't end with teabags either. Until recently the sea was considered fair game. Most of us drew the line at plastics, somehow realising early on that these just wouldn't do, but since the majority of materials would degrade back to their element atoms given time, we did some outrageous things. It wasn't that we were bad people. We just didn't know any better. Once far enough away at sea to be sure they wouldn't wash up on the nearest beach, many decent family men lobbed glass bottles and tin cans overboard in the belief that until they dissolved back to sand or iron oxide they might provide a cosy home for some small creature.

This flawed assumption gave me the answer to a problem when I delivered a motorsailer to the French Riviera back in the 1970s. To boost fuel capacity I'd lashed three 45-gallon oil drums into the cockpit. They proved a Godsend on passage, but they did little for the ambience as my crew and I sipped our cocktails stern-to the fashionable dock at sundown. The problem was that although they were well and truly empty, the otherwise excellent harbour board had failed to provide a suitable waterfront rubbish dump. Despite irrational hopes to the contrary they wouldn't just go away, and when the owner wrote to announce his imminent arrival, the time came for direct action.

My shipmates and I put to sea early the next morning, cruised out until the Alpes Maritimes were a hazy line, then rolled the offending containers across the rail with their bungs out. Needless to say, they floated, and as we motored away across the blue Mediterranean an early dawning of ecological accountability began nagging at my insides. My mate clearly felt the same.

'You'll have to sink them, Skipper,' he said bluntly.

For a moment I considered passing the buck, but he was a strong-minded fellow and I knew he'd give me short shrift. Sinking oil drums fell into the same category as fixing the heads. It's the skipper or nobody. So we turned around and I dived in amongst them armed with a heavy marline spike. I punched enough holes in the first one to let the air out, then wrapped my arms around it and forced it under. It rolled and bubbled as it resisted my efforts to finish it off, but after a few minutes the struggles diminished in proportion to decreasing buoyancy until finally it sank and I turned my attention to its companions.

I had blonde hair when I perpetrated this environmental atrocity and I'm snow-white now, so I like to imagine that my shame has rusted away to nothing a mile down in that deep water. Maybe it has, perhaps it hasn't, but what's important is that, only half a lifetime later, mankind's sense of responsibility has advanced so far that I cringe to think I could have done such a thing.

I changed my engine oil last weekend. As always, I carried the old oil ashore to the tank provided by my local marina. I was just about to toss the well-emptied can into the adjacent skip when I noticed an unusual example of human enlightenment that stopped me in my tracks. A sign announced a list of items suddenly banned from this erstwhile take-all depository. Some were relevant, others perplexing. I could cope with 'oil filters and half-full paint cans', but an interdict on tipping empty ones seemed harsh. 'Engines and fuel tanks' suggested that the skip was patronised by sailors of super-human strength; 'detonators and unexploded ordnance' might have been better expressed as 'out-of-date flares' which are always a temptation and didn't get a mention, while 'printed-circuit boards' was unkind, because the echo sounder I'd salvaged from the same tip 20 years previously had served me well.

Mysteriously, all drums had to have their labels removed, but the most obtuse items on the disqualified list had to be 'radioactive materials' and 'Japanese knotweed'.

No suggestions were offered as to where any of these could now be dropped, so I suppose the night-time woodlands are alive with stealthy yachtsmen fly-tipping junk from the barred list such as 'cases of artillery shells', 'waste from abattoirs' and 'dead animals'.

Makes you long for the good old days of teabag flipping doesn't it?

FEELING THE PINCH

When times are hard it is worth deciding what
onboard kit is really valuable

One of the last true areas of privacy in the Western world is the
loo, and haven't they come on in our lifetimes? I'm advised
that even the better North of England grammar schools now
feature cubicle doors which lock. Not only does this deliver the shy
from the ridicule of the unkind, it enables the inmates to read whatever
they choose without interruption. From scraps gathered at boat show
appearances, many seafaring readers favour a Cunliffe text book for
those daily minutes of solitude, but in these difficult times, my own
choice of short-span literature is a work by Richard Browning entitled
'How to survive the Credit Crunch'. Amongst useful tips about avoiding
motorway service stations and knocking off the booze, I found a jewel
entitled, 'Do I really need this?' Mr Browning was wondering whether
to spring for that expensive Mexican patio heater he'd always wanted
which was now on offer at half-price, but my mind had moved on to
the latest generation of electronic chart plotters.

Those of us who enjoy this method of navigation are hugely blessed in comparison to our predecessors. You'll recall the history. It all started back in the mid-1990s with monochrome vector charts on tiny screens. Even if you could understand them, you couldn't discern detail unless it was pitch dark and then you couldn't find the buttons to make them work. Those early sets were virtually useless, yet they were the trail-blazers of the only total revolution in navigation since 1761, when Harrison's chronometer brought longitude to every seaman who could add up. For the first time, a skipper could see a real-time fix, while a projection of his recent positions showed visually where the vessel was actually tracking. It didn't take many years to progress from these primitive beginnings to plotters with bright screens, user-friendly programs and charts that are clear and comprehensive. Soon, such benefits as AIS and radar overlays were added. Every time-honoured problem was now solved. What more could a sensible navigator ask?

The most relevant answer to this question is, I suppose, bigger screens. They'd be good, wouldn't they, because the thorniest issue of the modern chart plotter isn't that we can't read it or that the software was written by the Man in the Moon. The sorry truth is that while even a small paper chart measures over 2ft 6in × 1ft 6in, my biggest plotter screen is only 12 inches across the diagonal. Anything bigger than that gets seriously expensive and guzzles far more battery power than we small-yacht sailors can afford. As a result, we still have to live with the zooming and panning challenges that have bedevilled these otherwise wonderful machines from the start. Instead of some serious R&D into this vital area, the suppliers are in grave danger of losing the plot – as one might say. The latest stream of equipment is classic fodder for Richard Browning. For more money, we are now encouraged to invest in 'added value' charts that purport to show the world of cartography in three dimensions. We can tilt the display to view our destination from a variety of angles, with little lights that blink on and off just like the real thing and are equally bewildering. The most alarming element about approaching strange harbours after dark for many of us is the wall-to-wall flashing lights. These, of course, are made even more obscure by ambient illumination from the shore – pub signs, fairgrounds, occasionally even an adventurously lit sign of unambiguous promise, 'Gents'. More likely, these days, it'll say, 'Male', offering a depressing insight into the anticipated clientele, but it distracts our gaze from the main event just the same. What I want from my chart is a bird's-eye view that removes all this confusion – a precise, 2-D delivery that dishes up the essential information, and no more. It's called an Admiralty Chart, or its uncluttered electronic equivalent.

The alarming thing about some of these new features is that people believe in them unquestioningly. I had a yarn recently with a yachtsman who described passing through a tiny, rock-strewn channel using only his 3-D charts to watch his keel clearing the obstructions. His alternative was a visual transit that has served mariners for centuries.

'How did your route compare with the transit?' I enquired.

'Oh, that's old hat now. I didn't bother to look. . . .'

I asked myself whether the surveyor of his chart had indicated the smoothly undulating plane connecting the 3-D soundings on the screen, or whether a creative cartographer had filled in the gaps with a computer. I love electronic navigation and I admire the instruments now at our disposal, but one thing was certain. Whoever created that chart hadn't made the sort of effort traditional cartographers put in to draw a user's eye to the transit. The bottom line seems to be that in the frantic search for new developments in the face of fierce competition, money is being invested in trivia while work on what would truly help is not in evidence.

Manufacturers tell me that people adore these gimmicks. I don't doubt that some do, but Browning's question, 'Do I really need this,' will sound loudly in the ears of many. The Irish writer Flann O'Brien summed up the matter in 1939.

'When money's tight and hard to get, and your horse has also ran,

'When all you have is a heap of debt, a pint of plain is your only man.'

He could have been talking about chart plotters and hard times. The word from my heads compartment is that there is much in what he says.

RECKONING WITH DOUBT

Putting too much trust in a single navigational source is asking for trouble

Last week I bumped into a fellow Ocean Yachtmaster examiner who was being robbed of his beauty sleep by some of his fast-track candidates. None had completed a real ocean voyage; instead, they'd made 600-mile trips aboard skippered yachts in the Caribbean. The way the rules stand, this is enough to qualify, and the distance doesn't have to be a rhumb line between ports so long as most of it is more than 50 miles from land. These guys had been milking the system to the full by nipping out from some palmy bay, running half their distance across the trade wind with the islands below the horizon, then returning to some likely shelter for a swift rum. One thing you can be confident of in the West Indies is plenty of sunshine, so finding enough of this valued commodity to dash off the required sights posed no problem.

You might not think much of this as a way of achieving Ocean status, but my colleague's insomnia wasn't being caused by the RYA's minimum passage requirements. It was about unalterable navigational axioms and his concerns apply to us all.

This isn't a technical piece, so if celestial sights aren't your bag, don't worry. They flagged up the issue, however, so here's a rapid run-down on how they work. Hang in for the next couple of paragraphs and you'll see the point.

A noon sight serves up a latitude. It doesn't require an accurate time check, but it doesn't produce a fix either. You use your sextant to measure the sun's altitude when it stops rising in the middle of the day, work a simple sum, and Bob is your uncle. Unfortunately, there isn't an equally handy method for longitude. For this, you must shoot the sun two or three hours before noon, note the precise time, and work a slightly more complicated sum. Significantly, this relies on a dead reckoning position (DR) as its starting point. Its position line (PL) runs at an angle across the chart. You log the sight, then toddle off for a kip until it's time to clamber up for the noon latitude and the big result.

Because you log the noon sight too, you have a distance and a course steered between two sights. This enables you to 'run up' the forenoon sight just as you would for an old-fashioned running fix. The point at which the transferred PL intersects the latitude is the noon position.

You'll appreciate that an inexperienced person peering through an unfamiliar Victorian instrument while balancing on a plunging deck like a rodeo rider is unlikely to produce a result of notable accuracy. My own sun sights are rarely within two miles of our true position. Looking at candidates' workings, I have found discrepancies of up to thirty. Such things happen, and an examiner makes his own judgement, but it wasn't lack of accuracy that was bothering my chum. His alarm bells were ringing because the students had apparently been taught that, having plotted a forenoon sight, they should immediately move their DR up to the new PL. These guys were so uncomfortable with an honest DR that they were modifying it by grabbing at the straw of an unconfirmed single source of data (the forenoon PL).

The DR had begun life the previous day at a location which, for all its potential sins, was at least a running fix. If they had further refined this with an afternoon sight, they would have been starting from a three-point cocked hat. To 'adjust' the DR a mere twenty hours later on the basis of a solitary PL which might be well adrift is worrying. It suggests that, lacking the assurance that GPS navigation had given them from the outset of their training, the candidates, or perhaps even their teachers, were thoroughly uneasy without it.

Working with 'areas of probability' has been the meat and drink of ocean navigators from the beginning of time, and they should have been using their new forenoon PL to begin to query the DR – if danger loomed and the sight suggested they were nearer the rocks than the DR indicated, they could act accordingly; in mid-ocean, any discrepancy would do no more than raise an eyebrow, and so on. Such concepts were obviously unknown to these GPS-dedicated minds, yet as soon as the screens go blank, they are still the only thing we have.

What frightens me is that these potential professional skippers apparently have no notion of two essentials of navigation.

1. Always demand data from more than a single source.
2. An in-depth strategy for handling genuine uncertainty should be so burned into the soul that it clicks in automatically when required.

I've seen some excellent Yachtmasters produced by fast-tracking, but there's more to skippering than cramming for an exam. Only the mindset that comes with genuine command experience can develop appropriate reactions to the once-common phenomenon of not knowing where we are. Navigating with uncertainty remains a far cry from those quirky historical issues that no longer concern mainstream sailors, such as beating to windward in square rig or turning in a racking seizing. The apparently obscure issue raised by my fellow-examiner is actually a clear warning shout.

FOR YOUR COMFORT
AND SAFETY

Understand new crew's concerns and pre-empt
their fears – after all, you were a novice once

Last week I came home from America with BA on the dreaded
night flight. The dinner was reasonable, the wine plentiful, the
so-called sleep virtually non-existent and the breakfast awful, but
the cabin staff were exemplary. One way and another, the experience
beat the daylights out of my last North Atlantic sailing passage – until
we landed and the PA system delivered a piped message telling us to
stay in our seats until the aircraft was moored on its stand. Anybody
with half a brain would see the logic of this. The prospect of folks
cannoning into one another and bouncing off the bulkheads as they
dodge the avalanches of duty-free booze from the overhead stowage
boxes doesn't bear thinking about, to say nothing of the need to keep
gangways clear for the professionals. A polite order to remain seated
would be plenty, but it was not to be. The Health and Safety Executive
have weaselled their way into the otherwise rational world of flying, so

the disembodied voice advised us that to comply was 'for our comfort and safety'.

What utter baloney! That it was for our safety was so obvious it should have gone without saying but, sure as gales in January, it had nothing to do with our comfort. After sitting for seven hours, my over-long frame was craving to stand up. The moronic statement patronised everyone, including the cabin staff. They must find it embarrassing unless, like most sensible people, they switch off as soon as they hear the ludicrous cant strike up.

In case by now you're wondering what on earth this has to do with yachting, the thought was triggered by an exchange of emails yesterday. My correspondent was perplexed because, while he himself had never been emotionally troubled by his boat heeling, his guests and his wife were not blessed with his confidence. To put it bluntly, their fear that the 35ft yacht would fall over was spoiling everyone's day. His knowledge of basic physics was more than adequate to explain how this could never happen in the Solent on a summer afternoon, but the rational arguments weren't helping. He wondered if he was alone in his problem, or whether I had come across the fear of capsize elsewhere.

Oddly enough, I had – on every Competent Crew course I ever ran with novices. Dealing with it turned out not to be so difficult, because the earliest person I found suffering from it was me.

The first time I ever set a sail there was no instructor. I was with a friend on a 22ft gaff sloop. She'd been chartered for us by our fathers on the Norfolk Broads, perhaps hoping the experience might do us some unspecified good. I had never been in a sailing boat in my life. We'd read a book, we were 14 years old, it was blowing Force 6 and the yacht had no engine.

I remember being surprised by how big the sails looked, how noisy it all was before they were sheeted in, and how totally disorientated I felt when my world tipped onto its side. Subsequent experience while training others taught me to deal with these by a pre-emptive policy. Before I start hoisting, I casually explain about the alarm-generating factors ('I remember the first time I did this, I didn't half give myself a shock! Etc. ...'). In particular I describe my own early reactions to the impression that the sky was falling on top of me. Next comes the undeniable fact that it hasn't done so yet, and the lively hope that it won't start today. Our boat is as secure as the next one. They're all stabilised by their ballast. Besides, if any of them toppled from wind alone, Nelson would never have ruled the waves and Noah's Ark would have inverted off Mount Ararat. That would have finished off mankind at an early date and the issue would never have arisen.

I also invite first-timers to look around at other boats, concentrating on the ones that are heeling heavily. I try to relate what we're seeing to the experience they are about to have, remembering that things always feel downright dramatic until you get used to it. We are, after all, creatures of *terra firma*, and we're hot-wired to keep our feet below our heads.

When we finally sheet in and stomachs are taking that first big lurch, I make reassuring noises, recalling the boat we were watching. If she's still available for observation and still the right way up, so much the better.

There's more, though. From time to time, many of us sail with crew of an unusually nervous disposition, and 'Hands up' anyone who doesn't occasionally drive the boat a bit harder than he should. I'm no better than the rest. I can be a bit of a maritime petrol-head when it comes to carrying sail, especially if I've a full crew to drag it down. Given this personal insight, I've learned to observe knuckles for whiteness and eyes for the flickerings of incipient panic. At the first signs of anxiety I stop thinking about my own fun and shorten down in good time, involving my crew heavily in the process. While I'm at it, I bolster up morale by advising the team that this is for their comfort, not their safety! Contrary to the propaganda pumped at us day by day, the two are not necessarily synonymous.

GRIEF RELIEF

Avoid these sailing sins and you'll live to crew another day

'**B**aby, Baby, you're out of time. . . .' sang Cliff my watch mate, not quite under his breath for the tenth time that night. 'Out of tune more likely,' I thought. 'Why not finish the song, or better still shut up?'

This was many years ago and we were unhappy deckhands on a large, beaten-up vessel. Even with hindsight I can find no excuse for our skipper, a paranoid hater of his fellow men; the mate exhibited archetypal symptoms of manic depression, and the cook seemed on remittance from Hell. We focsle hands had every reason to be nice to one another, yet even in our small world the atmosphere was strained. These days I can see that Cliff probably loathed the way I left my kit lying around but, like so many before me, I fancied myself without sin.

There are all sorts of explanations for the old superstition of never whistling on board, including whistling up a headwind, but I'm convinced the truth is about cabin fever. We can't escape our companions on a long passage, and they are well stuck with us. A snatch of tune done to death is only one of many things that can ignite the human tinderbox. Seamanship books are disgracefully lacking in advice for dealing with a shipmate ripe for a punch on the nose, but never fear. Here are a few selected extracts from *Cunliffe's Little Book of Aggro*.

THE MOROSE CREWMAN

Women don't seem to suffer from this problem, but a classic sign of impending conflict on an extended passage is when a chap becomes uncharacteristically quiet and introspective. If he has a wife or partner back home, this is usually a case of 'cherchez la femme'. Either he's feeling bad because he's having fun and she's out paying the mortgage, or he's convinced himself that she is even now having her wicked way with the gardener. Your dying duck will sap crew morale as surely as a Jonah, so you are duty-bound to take steps. Often, the best answer is somehow to get Mister Misery talking. It's a lonely world when you're worried, and most unhappy people can't wait to cough up once they find a friend. Having rooted out the problem you can at least reassure the victim. Remind him that his gardener is an ugly weirdo, tell him his wife will be enjoying the extra 'space', but whatever you do, recognise the signs and react.

THE BAD-MANNERED SAILOR

Manners exist to help us live together without driving one another nuts. They therefore take on exceptional importance at sea. When my daughter was still an infant, I shipped a young crewman who used to pick up his plate and lick it clean at the end of dinner. Call me middle-class, but this wasn't what I wanted the child to grow up doing. The lad displayed a wide array of unacceptable antics which first irritated, then angered me. It took a while for me to work up to slipping him a firm word away from the rest of the company, but once I bit the bullet I was surprised at how readily he accepted the advice to clean up his act. I was spared a stretch in jail for violent crime and began there and then to examine my own behaviour more critically. I hope I've learned from him.

THE ALIENATED SOUL

People rapidly grow alienated when their aspirations fail to concur. A ship can only be in one place at a time, so if two parties want something different, one will be disappointed. Not having the option of walking away, the aggrieved party becomes glum, aggressive, sarcastic, or otherwise unpleasant. A typical cause is inviting a guest for a jolly week's harbour-hopping, then staying at sea in filthy weather instead. And what about the teenager up for an afternoon's shopping in Cherbourg when you want to drift downtide hooking mackerel? A compromise must be found.

My favourite solution to frustrated wishes was dreamed up by a crew who successfully circumnavigated from South Africa. At the outset they thrashed out where they would go, who would be responsible for what, and how much each would pay. Then they wrote it down and signed it. When the first rumblings of trouble sounded somewhere in the Pacific, the skipper dug out the agreement. End of problem.

WHISTLING

As a postscript I must return to this evil habit. It's the repetition of a disembodied phrase that annoys, and most people don't even know they're doing it.

Not long ago I was shaving in the gents at a marina down-Channel. My trip with Cliff and the misanthropic skipper with his mad mate was 30 years gone when a voice I seemed to know began humming from behind a shower curtain.

'Baby, Baby, you're out of time. . . .'

I was still slumped over the basin when the curtain flicked aside to reveal a grey-haired, stouter Cliff. There was nothing for it but to buy him a beer, and it was then I found I'd been wrong about him all along. He might have been a lousy singer, but he didn't hesitate to stand the second round. By the third pint, we were laughing about that awful cook. 'Never hold a grudge' isn't bad advice either.

PUT YOUR MONEY AWAY

A costly Christmas berth begs the question as to whether British marinas are the unacceptable face of capitalism

Credit-crunched sailors with deep pockets and short arms visiting Cherbourg will be relieved to learn that they can still anchor outside the inner breakwater for free. I once made a policy of lying here and spending the marina dues with a man by the name of Henri who ran a well-stocked 'cave' on the quay. I had a stout fibreglass tender that rowed beautifully. The pull to town wasn't onerous and by securing the stem dinghy inside the locks my crew and I could load up in comfort. On one occasion, however, this admirable arrangement broke down.

The day was the sort of rainy one in which Normandy specialises, so we lingered longer than usual sampling Henri's finest. Staggering out with cases of the right stuff, we didn't notice that the tide had gone down. We loaded up the punt and rowed away, only to be brought up with a round turn by the lock gates. The lock keeper was eyeing us so balefully that nobody had the neck to ask him to open up. It looked as though we were stuck for the next six hours, until someone suggested 'portaging' the boat up a set of stone steps that led directly to the street. Reconnaissance revealed the local equivalent of a zebra crossing at the top, complete with traffic lights. On the far side, a second flight of weedy stairs descended to open water.

Dragging the boat up the steps was a struggle, but we managed it without unloading our cargo. At street level, we waited for the green man to light up, skidded our charge across the greasy wet cobbles, then launched her like a lifeboat in front of a crowd of bewildered French commuters. We rowed away into the gathering gloom, happy in the knowledge that we could drink the night away in the comfort of our complimentary berth.

At 0745 the following morning I popped my head out of the hatch and noted a fleet of yachts flying various British ensigns pouring out of the marina. These chancers were, of course, 'doing a runner' from the harbourmaster, whose representatives don't usually turn up with their ticket machines until coffee time. While this initiative represented a viable method of preserving a ship's liquidity, I wanted to visit this favourite harbour again. Because one can never be sure about not being spotted, I'm inclined these days either to pay up or anchor.

Pay up. Now, there's the rub! Over Christmas this year I was cruising on the Solent. My travels took me to Hythe Marina Village to share some good cheer with a couple of old chums who live there. I'd never entered this haven in my own boat before and, on the whole, marina villages are not my bag. Hythe, however, is different. It's been around long enough to mature. The so-called 'lifestyle' fantasy offered by agents for some such developments is notably absent and I've had some good times there.

Depending on your point of view, my boat is either a modern classic or an eccentric throwback to the gruesome days when wooden ships were sailed by iron men and neither had much fun out of it. She's 40 feet on deck with a sparred length of around 53 feet, although I can't swear to the latter because I've never bothered to measure up. Often, a sporting berthing master will find me a pontoon where my bowsprit can hang over nowhere land with no questions asked. So in I went, Christmas tree at my masthead, exuding bonhomie.

I stayed one night, saw my pals and trotted up to the lock in the morning to brass up. If you are a yacht owner, I recommend that you take a stiff drink before reading the next sentence, because you're going to need it. I was banged for – now get this – 58 quid.

I'm still so astounded that I don't really know what to say about this. Is it the unacceptable face of capitalism, perhaps, or maybe insane corporate greed in an era where nice people are going bust because they can't pay their bills? Whatever the cause, I can advise that in Sweden I recently cruised for six weeks, sometimes anchoring, sometimes berthing in town centres, at a cost of around £250. In Brittany last summer, one harbourmaster took a look at my boat and waived his reasonable fees because, he said, she improved his view. The result of sensible harbour dues is that sailors spend more money in the town and feel a whole lot better about the place. There's something rotten in dear old Blighty and I have only one answer.

Take a leaf from the log book of my friend, Dutch Rob. He loves the Channel as much as we do, and he beats down from Holland year after year with the target of staying all summer without paying a penny. His secret anchorages are numerous and delightful, he says, but he's keeping them to himself because he knows I'm a pilot-book writer.

That's next season's job then. See who can cruise for a fortnight, have fun, and pay the least. Over to you!

GOING SIDEWAYS FAST

It is easy to underestimate how the wind can blow a yacht sideways, but one touch of a button can make the picture clear

O ne autumn in those surprisingly recent years before GPS, I found myself walloping home to the Solent from Norway. Northwesterly 6 had been promised for the next couple of days. Not ideal, but we were under pressure from a large smoked salmon stowed in a locker on deck. Its purveyor had given it ten days maximum and that had been almost a week ago. The hands were determined to save it for an arrival celebration in Beaulieu, so I accepted more wind than I'd have liked and squared up to 600 miles of grey North Sea. Comfort would be in short supply for the living, but the mortal remains of the King of fish had a fighting chance.

Twelve hours out, the stiff breeze had increased to a moderate gale. The waves were building but we had a biggish boat and so far we were safe enough. You couldn't say the same the following night, with the wind at a steady 9 and the seas breaking regularly. We ran off for the bad ones, taking them on the quarter, then luffed back to course as best we could.

Progress was spectacular, but life on board was grim. There wasn't a dry spot to be had, and one of my shipmates had abandoned his bunk to doss on the cabin sole under a traditional full-length oilskin coat. The mate reported him dead at the midnight change of watch, but closer examination reassured that he was merely blue with cold. Each successive sea was throwing us solidly to leeward when I spoke with a passing Dutch coaster on the VHF. Like us, her skipper felt hard done-by over the weather. He was complaining that a light board had carried away from the bridge wing when a sickening lurch combined with a noise like a low-flying squadron of Tornadoes suggested that everything was far from well on my deck. A wail from the cockpit confirmed that I was not wrong.

'The bulwarks are gone skipper,' came the call, 'and the safety gear is on its way to Denmark...'

I checked the bilge, then signed off from my cosy chat, advising the Dutchman that although we had just suffered structural damage, we were making no more water than usual and were not at risk. I will never forget the seamanlike understatement of his final remark.

'What a pity. Out.'

Up in the real world, the escaping man-overboard strobe blinked once as both it and the boat hit neighbouring wave-tops a hundred yards apart. We never saw it again. I made a mental note to replace all such lights with fixed bulbs, then shone a torch on the wreckage of the ten-inch bulwarks. The oak capping rail had survived, but the boards were smashed to Kingdom Come. Not a splinter remained.

'How's the salmon?'

'Still there,' observed the watchman laconically, scrambling back into the cockpit after checking around the deck. 'I asked him what he thought, and he said that at least the green water will get away a bit quicker.'

The only notable benefit that came with the morning was an appearance by the sun at around coffee time. Peeping through the scud directly abeam, it allowed me to grab an ideal sight for assessing cross-track error. This was a concept unknown before electronic navigation, but we understood well enough what it meant to be off course. My dead reckoning, duly refined by the position line, indicated an astounding 17 degrees of leeway. Neither my life's experience nor any text book had prepared me for such excesses, but I hadn't been in the habit of storming along with a strong gale and a full ocean sea smack on the beam. My arithmetic stood up to closer examination, and I had confidence in my heading because, in those days of 'Lead, Log, Lookout and Trust in the Lord', swinging the compass was a priority. The seas really were shoving us a huge distance downhill. Without that sight, I'd have ended up on the beach in Germany rather than the Dover Strait.

Fortunately, the wind veered towards evening. We cracked on sail as it moderated, steered high enough to retrieve what we'd lost and fetched our berth in four days flat. The salmon gave its all, as did a bottle of malt someone produced, and I turned in with the uneasy feeling that I had been spared.

There was cause to reflect on this passage while crossing the Strait of Gibraltar earlier this year. Like many a hapless mariner thereabouts, I hadn't taken the tide, the current and my own leeway seriously enough. Visibility was poor and the wind strong, so I feared the worst. It was hard to observe visually what was happening to the yacht, and my predecessor at the diminutive plotter had either switched off the projected track or had never activated it. Leaving the watch on deck to their own devices, I invested a productive ten minutes trawling though the software until I managed to bring the function to life. Up came my track, an astounding 25 degrees to leeward of my ship's head. So much easier than working it all out from a sun sight and a log reading, and even more effective. I gritted my teeth, winched in the sheets, and made Morocco in time for supper.

One of the key features of a modern chart plotter is the probing arrowhead that foresees exactly where your boat will arrive if things stay as they are. It highlights unexpected cross-sets and leeway at a glance. It's easy to be lazy about using the full power of a plotter, especially an unfamiliar one on a chartered boat, but when I think how a sun sight was required to save my smoked salmon from inevitable decomposition, it seems rude not to take a little trouble when such wonders are on offer.

A LIFE OF LUXURY?

When it comes to sailing, the media just can't seem to get it right

Have you noticed how the non-specialist press and some script-writers display a talent for hyperbole, cliché and plain non-sense when they're talking about boats?

'Mr Bloggs was rescued today after being swept off his 30ft luxury yacht by a freak wave in Storm Force 7 winds inside Plymouth Breakwater. . .' This is not a direct quote from the Daily Blah. It's fabricated from three television news reports.

'Luxury yachts' do exist, I suppose, but I'd like to see a dictionary definition of what constitutes 'luxury' in the context of offshore sailing. Genuine freak waves certainly lurk out there in extreme weather. They're so far apart that few sailors ever meet one, but seas larger than average come along in most gales when two common-or-garden undulations happen to coincide. It doesn't make them freaks. A wave scientist could predict them, I'm sure, and all of us who've been out in a blow are well aware of how our world goes quiet every so often before the really big ones tumble into our cockpits. They are, however, no more freakish than an oak in deep woodland grown tall in its search for daylight.

As for 'Force 7 storms' and their friends and relations, you can only cry, can't you?

I started thinking about this the other night while watching a television drama-documentary about the sinking of the Cunard liner *Lusitania* by the German U20 in WWI. I was enjoying the drama side of the confection and was finding the historical aspects of interest until the ship slipped her lines. Then, despite the electronically generated views, the technicalities of the seafaring rapidly became so awful that I lost faith in everything else. Viewers were invited to credit a submarine northwest of Ireland steering something like 331 degrees in order to arrive off the southwest coast. We also saw the German crew charging around like balloons with the air escaping because an unarmed ship had suddenly been spotted in decent visibility at remarkably short range, but the best bit came when the Old Head of Kinsale was sighted from the liner following a period of fog. If that had indeed been the only feature in sight, a Merchant Navy captain surrounded by dab-hands at sextant operation with a copy of Norie's Tables in his bookshelf would have been in fat city. He didn't need GPS. He'd have wasted no time fixing his position with a bearing and a distance off the light – the bearing from his first-rate, corrected compass on the stable platform of a 32,000-tonner's bridge, and the range determined by vertical sextant angle on the lighthouse lantern. Very accurate he'd have been too. Not Captain Turner, however. This excellent officer became uncharacteristically aerated and demanded 'a four-point fix' on the lighthouse.

At this point, my wife burst out laughing. This was a shame, because I was trying my best to live with this guff and find out why the politicians had tried to hang the poor skipper out to dry following the sinking, but it was too late. I'd lost it too. What a pity. Any respectable Yachtmaster could have sorted out the rubbish after reading the otherwise excellent script once. The show took 90 minutes to watch, so I suppose by the time he'd written his report and cross-checked it the cost might have been a day of his time. Compared with the bankroll expended on recreating the ship's bridge and the insides of the U-boat, it would have been excellent value.

Compare this costly spectacular with the good old *Onedin Line* which many of us used to watch on Friday nights back in the 1970s. We all had a laugh as the hoary retainer, Captain Baines, clung to the wheel of the *Charlotte Rhodes* while the inevitable tempest raged. You could almost hear the fans generating the wind, and the seawater that lashed him looked suspiciously like buckets-full hove from stage left, but we didn't care. Directors couldn't do more in those days of miniscule budgets before computer graphics, but at least they didn't blunder over the obvious. When Anne Onedin taught the old boy to navigate by the heavens she did a pretty sound job, and our hearts rejoiced when the honest captain put the ambitious young owner straight about carrying too much sail in a rising gale. With the ship rounding up and his knuckles white as he ran out of helm at full lock, he finally spoke his mind:

'I can't hold her no more, Mr Onedin. . . . You'll have to take a reef in!'

The vessel was a topsail schooner, so I suppose they had the option of letting the mainsheet fly, but the crew were few in number, mutinous, and probably refreshing themselves at the studio bar. Any sailor could see that the two officers would never manage to haul the sail back in again. Good decision, Baines.

Now I've shifted that burden off the dead-man's chest, I'm away to my luxury yacht to catch the tide. I hope I don't make the news by being wiped out by a freak wave in the west Solent.

DON'T NEGLECT YOUR BOTTOM

Neglecting what went on below the waterline leads to a close call with a coral reef

'You buy a gallon of this, Young Man,' advised the chandler's runner in the market behind the Barbican. 'Only ten quid. It'll see you clean round the world!'

All manner of gear used to be available on the streets of Plymouth back in the early 1970s. I expect it had something to do with the thriving naval base and the financial creativity of the old-time dockyard matey.

'Feel the weight,' he continued, hefting the rusty, unlabelled can. 'More copper in that antifoul than there are rozzers down the nick!'

I sampled the displacement and, if quality were to be equated with mass, I was onto a winner. Besides, something about his broken nose and those hands like wicket-keeper's gloves inspired confidence. I accepted the merchandise, slipped him my last two fivers and tottered back to the boat.

After breakfast the following morning, I started stirring the sludge deep in the can; by coffee time I had something akin to melted chocolate, except that it was bright red. Applying the first layer was exhausting. Laying on the second left me in what felt like a terminal decline. Just before sunset, however, I was able to admire a slick bottom that I hoped might remain that way right down to the tropics.

Fifteen months, many thousands of miles and a number of underwater scrubs later, I decided to spend Christmas in the Hog Island anchorage at the Southern end of Grenada in the West Indies. The festivities were a spectacular success, with South Africans expertly barbecuing real sucking pigs on the beach, neat little barrels of rum, and beautiful girls. The sea was warm, unwanted sea-life prospered and I failed to realise that the pusser's antifouling had reached the end of its considerable tether. I stayed a month, but it was only when I finally hove in the hook and put the engine in gear that I realised how foul my boat had become. The propeller went round all right, but no encouraging whoosh of propwash followed, and no movement of boat through water either. There wasn't time to find out why as I began to drift, so I whizzed up the main and eased the sheet to bear away through the reefs. Instead of leaning sweetly to the tradewind and accelerating eagerly as she normally did, however, my little thoroughbred slid sideways like an old scow with the centreboard up.

As I ran off into the open sea to clear the leeward end of the island, I peered beneath the stern, looking for a half-ton of fishing net on my propeller, but nothing was apparent. Rounding Point Saline where the airport now is, I hauled my sheets to head north. As the first proper gust hit, I grabbed a rope's end and hung out like a trapezing dinghy crew to see under the boat. Not only were weed and barnacles sprouting in profusion, coral was forming just below the waterline. The propeller was a sort of grey ball where the polyps had established their main bridgehead.

There was no doubt about what I had to do. Rather than heading north for St Lucia as planned, I decided to beat up into St Georges and strike a deal with Frenchy, who owned the local slipway. Close-hauled, the boat hardly moved, so I stood in to a rocky stretch of shore on the port tack. Leaving things to the last minute as I often did in those days, I shoved the helm down with breakers in sight. The boat had never yet missed stays on me, but laminar flow was now no more than a distant memory. She refused to tack not once but twice, so rather than risk a third debacle I gybed her round. The coral was inches below the keel in the crystal water and by the time the boom finally crashed over, the crayfish were eyeing me hopefully as they queued up to nibble at my bones. I never want to come as close to a reef again.

There is no room here to recount the experience of hauling with the hand winch on Frenchy's dilapidated cradle, but it served its purpose. The boat was so foul it was little wonder I had almost lost her. It took two days to scrape and sand her clean. Finding an affordable gallon of the right stuff proved a sterner challenge than in Plymouth, but in the end I swapped a bunch of old shackles for a bucket-full. It looked a bit thin, but Frenchy assured me it would be improved by adding a pound of his wife's special chilli powder. This ecologically sound adjustment was quickly made and the paint worked surprisingly well.

The moral of this true story is not an 'in-your face' conclusion about coral growth, or a recommendation to spike sophisticated modern antifouling with Old Mother Patak's curry paste. Like most of us, my life is no longer so extreme. Instead, it's about the creeping loss of performance that slinks up as the season runs on. Even a layer of slime is enough to slow us down, never mind the weed and barnacles. We spend good money on sails to extract that bit extra from our boats, yet without a clean bottom, as the singer Donovan might have observed back in 1965, we may as well try and catch the wind.

WHAT A STITCH UP!

Santa's Christmas message suggests it's time to give the hands a good whipping

I wonder what Father Christmas has lined up for your stocking this year? If your luck's in, one of his more sympathetic pixies will have parcelled up a bottle of 20-year-old Malt to cram into the business end. If those guys treat you anything like me, however, it's more likely to be a diary, a dodgy old tangerine and a couple of dried-out walnuts.

My family always spend Christmas Eve on board. After dinner we peg up the seaboot socks over the bogey stove, the wife awards me a nightcap that could stun a horse, the youngsters slide off ashore somewhere and I am laid to rest in my bunk up forward. I've never worked out who executes the miracle, but somehow the woolly footwear gets well stuffed some time between turning in and first light when I crawl out to the galley humming a Christmas carol. As I riddle the fire and shove the kettle onto the heat, I check up on whether the tireless old saint has accepted the glass of Tio Pepe and the cold mince pie left out for him. It's always disappeared except for a crumb or two. Last year, he went so far as to leave a note of thanks on the back of his napkin. I turned up the oil lamp on the saloon table. Rather equivocally, it read,

'Ta for the goodies. Sorry presents rubbish, but it's been a rough year in Greenland. Elves on strike, reindeer turning up noses at shortage of snow, unwelcome visit around mid-summer from tourists off big white ship. Luv, Santa.'

'PS,' it concluded, 'Your shorelines are a disgrace.'

That struck me right where it hurts. I'd recently equipped with some flashy modern multiplait to replace the four three-strand monsters I'd bought a decade ago from the fishermen's co-op in Peterhead. They had one great advantage in addition to the popular price tag. At 40ft long and well over an inch in diameter, their colossal dimensions kept them quiet in the fairleads. They never once robbed me of my rest by creaking all night, unlike those mingy little pieces of 12mm you get handed in raft-ups. The new ones were over-size as well, but, being polyester I hadn't bothered to whip the ends. Instead, I'd settled for the chandler burning them off with his hot knife. They hadn't unravelled, so I couldn't complain, but Father Christmas was obviously a thorough-going sailorman. He'd spotted my shame even in the dark.

Red-faced, I shoved a hand into my warm, dry stocking for a rootle around as the kettle started to sing. Out came the usual parade of unlikely items: a slab of Kendal Mint Cake – very tasty; a pair of knitted gloves with no fingers he must have found in the Salvation Army in Upernavik – OK for Steptoe senior, not much use in a gale offshore; the ritual Jaffa orange and a bag of 'Big D' nuts sporting a notably stimulating image of a young lady. Finally, near the bottom, I discovered a sailmaker's palm and a tube of new needles.

How could he have known what I needed? My sail needles had been looking sorry for themselves for years and I'd been searching for a palm ever since mine finally blew out the previous summer. This Old Faithful had been my companion all my sailing life and it owed the world nothing, but when the iron finally fell out of it I had to admit the thing had become dangerous. As I trudged off to dump it in the boatyard skip, I remembered with a heavy heart how it had punched through six layers of tabling to re-stitch the bolt-rope onto my canvas mainsail halfway between Canada and Ireland, and the way it had herring-boned a darn across four panels that had given up the ghost in despair. Since that black day, I'd been haunting chandleries, boat jumbles and Internet sites in search of a proper replacement, but all I found was 'Mickey Mouse' junk. Santa and his little helpers must have had special insight to lay hands on this one, but as soon as I saw it in the dim light, I knew it was a winner. My thumb fitted into the hole as though it had been tailored in Saville Row, the iron was securely fixed at just the correct angle, while the leather, tough without being too hard, promised that it would sooner feature in my will than give up in the meantime.

I made the tea, delivered the mugs to various Christians dotted around the ship who had not yet awakened to salute the happy morn, then took my prizes back to the bunk for closer inspection. Among the shiny new needles was an interesting bent one. I'd never seen such a thing before. I slipped on the palm and was trying to imagine what I might use it for when my wife, from what had appeared to be a deep and dreamless sleep, opened one eye for the last word.

'I think you'll find that after you've finished using that kit to tidy the dock-line ends, the curved needle will be ideal for stitching up the turkey and holding in the stuffing.'

By what feminine intuition, I asked myself, had she worked it all out so neatly.

Merry Christmas!

DON'T READ ALL
ABOUT IT

It's tempting to fill the cockpit full of instruments, but it's often better to develop your feel for the boat

'Could you move away from the instruments, please?' asked the helmsman edgily, acutely aware that he was being examined for his Yachtmaster's ticket. The 35-footer was losing way on a close reach as she approached a man-overboard dummy floating bravely in the sunshine. A crew member whose proportions suggested a day job with the Pontypool front row was taking a while to shift himself, and by the time he had shunted across to reveal a typical bank of dials, we were travelling so slowly that the keel stalled. The boat slid sideways into the 'no-go' zone leaving the 'victim' bobbing mockingly in the wind's eye.

A second crack at a man-overboard exercise is common enough to make these proceedings unmemorable. What blew my mind was that as the skipper bore off to beat back to the dummy, he excused himself on the grounds that he had been unable to read the boat speed. This singular announcement shook me to the soles of my wellies because the last thing on my mind at that point would have been clocking the numbers on an electronic readout. After all, taking way off under sail preparatory to rounding up is all about spilling wind until the helm goes spongy. This signals that the keel is losing its grip. If there is still some distance to travel, the mainsheet can be pulled back in just enough to re-establish control, and so on until the final judgement call when the boat is terminally stalled with the rudder hard to weather. She then scuffs off the last of her way and stops, not quite head-to-wind.

The critical velocity that defines the edge of the stall varies with conditions and the nature of the yacht herself, but whatever its numerical value may be, you know you're there because of the onset of lee helm. Spotting it in practice has nothing to do with the readout from a speed log.

One weekend last summer, I was racing in a club regatta with a novice skipper. It was a gusty old day and as mainsail trimmer I was obliged to 'dump' the sail from time to time to keep the boat on her feet and driving fast, especially when close-hauled. This sort of behaviour is common in modern cruisers, and I soon found that by watching the skipper at the wheel I could second-guess when to ease the sail. As we heeled, the helm went over and I could feel the boat slowing under the increased drag of the rudder. As I eased the traveller car down to leeward the helm returned towards the centreline. Speed was back up in no time; the skipper and I were soon anticipating and working as a team.

Later, the breeze fell away, giving me a welcome break from my labours, but windward progress wasn't as smooth as it could have been. Now and again the boat would sail a touch high for half a minute, or maybe she would sag off the breeze. Speed either fell off, or we heeled over more and made good less ground. You'd have felt both with your eyes shut. Initially, I put it down to a long trick at the wheel and short lapses of concentration, but I was wrong. Concerned to get the best from his boat, the skipper had started staring into the instruments on the binnacle pedestal. Each time he took his eyes off the sails, his feel for the helm lost its edge and progress took a dive.

Now, I'm not saying that cruising boats should have no instrumentation, but I do wonder about their universal relevance to everyday sailing. Even the requirement for a cockpit boat-speed readout is worth questioning. Racing is one thing, 'the max' being assumed. On a cruising boat, how hard we push is more often a compromise between the theoretically possible and what we settle for. It's all about comfort, stress management and our personal level of honest laziness. No need for a dial to tell us the bottom line on any of those.

The same goes for wind instrumentation. Top competition boats demand it because their computers specify sail changes by its readouts. We cruisers can afford to be less rigorous. You can't argue with the fact that it is safe to be able to work out what the speed of a following breeze might be if we decide to beat into it, but it doesn't take many years' experience to make this sort of judgement for ourselves. As for wind direction, we don't have to be Ben Ainslies to tell when a boat is on the verge of a gybe without using a clock. A masthead pointer does the trick nicely; so does a burgee, or even a glance at the air ruffling the water. Close-hauled after dark, it's all about the general awareness. On a wild midnight run, it's the same as it has always been unless you have a tricolour to light up the windex – that 'feel' factor again, plus the wind fingering your neck.

Instruments have their place, but over-reliance on them for data which may readily be acquired and processed using the senses we were born with can be counter-productive. Next time your skipper tells you to clear his view of the dials, I should consider the enjoyable option of mutiny and ask if he really needs to see them!

OWNING OR
BEMOANING?

Does the soft option of chartering outweigh pride of ownership?

On the face of things, it's hard to argue with a man who says, 'I spent my main holiday chartering in the Caribbean, then backed it up with a couple of odd weeks in Croatia.' Very nice too – especially if, like me, you've had a busy year and only managed a fortnight cruising in home waters. And it's not only work that has kept my feet dry. Even my boat chisels away so insidiously at my sea time that it sometimes makes me wonder about the benefits of ownership, until some incident crops up to remind me why I bother.

Back in September I was rubbing down my toerail one breezy morning when a gent came trundling past the mooring towards the sea.

'I bet you'd rather be sailing!' he wisecracked.

Anyone with brightwork to attend to gets a lot of this, and we all develop our own responses.

'Oh, it's not so bad. Besides, it'll be wet and windy out there.'

After he'd chugged off I returned to my sanding, but he'd made me think. I tend to keep my boats for many years, and the longer I have them, the more of myself I invest in them. Servicing literally everything, dealing with failures as they arise, devising improvements, being proud when she shines and ashamed when I let her down, all enrich my sailing. A big spin-off for hands-on ownership is that tackling jobs yourself makes the boat safer at sea because you generally have the right tools to hand and can deal with the unexpected more effectively than someone who sees the boat as disposable. I was genuinely appalled when a yacht I recently hired for a job carried no worthwhile tool kit.

'We don't want charterers messing about with our boats. . . .'

'So what if I blow something as basic as a cooling-water impeller? The anchor is only toy.'

'Call us on your mobile. We'll send someone to fix you up.'

I suppose I should be grateful that the coding authorities have ensured that I'm equipped with every known device to save me when the shortfall in real equipment has run me into danger. Call me old-fashioned, but. . . .

This 'rent-a-car' attitude is a far cry from six guys I've been working with to present the world with a little 'reality TV'. Each is a boat-owner, and all have had major problems to overcome during the summer if they are to get any sailing in before winter. There are two yachts that *YM* readers will immediately relate to, plus a 1930s dinghy, a 70-year-old clinker-built work boat and a water-jet speed boat of unknown origins bought apparently by mistake at an auction in the middle of Yorkshire. Everybody is strapped for cash, deadlines loom and the pressure's on in a big way. Apart from yours truly, the *dramatis personae* include a 'man-who-can' with a scrapyard in his back garden, two brothers-in-law testing their family ties alongside their technical skills, a company director with the soul of an engineer, a Thames river-man and a sailing chef. The producer gives them the respect they richly deserve as their fortitude is plumbed to the depths.

If you want to find out how they make out, you'll have to tune in to the ten-part series, but I can tell you that one of the most important lessons learned is that the more you put into a boat, the more you'll get out in the end. The chef's yacht is a wooden classic he buys to live aboard and go long-term cruising. When he discovers serious structural deterioration he thinks his world is falling in around him, but he digs deep and finds more shot in the locker of his personality than he ever realised. He fronts up to the truly depressing task of ripping out perfectly sound furniture to get at the horrors, then develops the technical know-how by squeezing every hour he can from the dreamland between his job and far too little sleep. Things grow far worse than he feared before they start to improve but, long before the show is over, this remarkable young man observes that whatever happens at sea, he'll know how to deal with it. He also says that if the boat turns out as he hopes, the way he'll feel as he sets out down his local creek is something you'd never equal by chartering in the world's most exotic location.

With luck, most of us will never have to face such severe tests, but I can't watch this band of quiet heroes struggling with their personal demons without finding my spirits lifted. As they battle through, they give me a series of reflections against which to judge my own lifestyle. Time was when I sometimes wondered whether owning a boat was really worth the grief. I don't any more.

FAIL SAFE

The battle for the right to go sailing without needless interference is well worth fighting

A long time ago I sailed to America with my wife. I'd imagined a land of clear, wide avenues lined with skyscrapers or classic colonial-style buildings. It wasn't like that at all when we came ashore at a backwoods creek in South Carolina. Instead, we found a rickety old dock supporting a cast of characters straight from Steinbeck's *Cannery Row*. Crab fishermen, out-of-work hippies and 'busted-flat' yachtsmen subsisted side by side, kept going by their sense of humour more than any hope of improvement. We were down on our luck too, so we fitted in well. One morning, a sweet girl who lived on a tiny wooden yacht turned out in a T-shirt that said it all. 'Isn't this a lovely day? Just watch some bastard louse it up!'

I'm reminded of that T-shirt as I read more and more official recommendations about our 'safety'. This obsession seems to be a world-wide phenomenon, not just one confined to Britain. Over in the States this year, the US Department of Homeland Security and the Coast Guard

157

are crusading to have all 'boaters' take a test to become 'certified'. The certificates will, US sailors are assured, help them to prove their identity.

It's hard to see how showing ID beyond what one is probably already carrying will shield anyone from drowning, so I hope our Stateside shipmates are greeting this piece of humbug with the, 'Nice try, Boys!' it deserves. However, every time officials in a credible foreign land start muttering about certification to improve safety on the water, it's a solemn matter for us all. The problem invariably is that when one person comes to grief in a rare leisure boating accident, those whose job it is to analyse and correct our behaviour are obliged to do something. To maintain perspective, it pays to consider the statistics.

What we all know and lands-people don't realise, is that going to sea is far less dangerous than the hack down the motorway to get to our yachts. Boat US, a body that looks after American sailors' interests, has done us a good turn here. Their researches into the annual figures indicate that, 'more people die in bathtubs and swimming pools than in recreational boats,' and that, 'operating a boat is far safer than riding a bicycle.' You also have much greater chance of perishing from falling out of bed, a chair or down the stairs than you do in tumbling from a boat.

So that's it, then. In case any legislator reading this is dreaming of a law to enforce wearing lifejackets on the water at all times, he'd save more lives regulating personal hygiene in the home. The whole nation would benefit from making it an arrestable offence to hop into a steaming tub in the privacy of one's own bathroom without wearing a lifer.

This sort of nonsense aside, we clearly should take our survival seriously. It's our duty as animals to try to stay alive. The instinct is inbuilt. We can't escape it and, what's more, we aren't entirely stupid. We sailors generally self-educate. Anyone who reads YM can't help keeping up with innovations to help us recover crew who've taken an unscheduled plunge, or ways of alerting the emergency services when our own attempts to save ourselves have foundered. We also know that lifejackets have improved light years from those awful old WWII hangovers that we wouldn't have been seen dead in unless the ship were going down. Today's units are so unobtrusive that any skipper can make a strong argument for wearing them deflated all the time we're on deck, but whether we do so or not must remain up to us individually. The situation is simply not parallel to seat belts in cars. If you lined up all the poor paramedics who've had to deal with road accidents beside their RNLI equivalents, the lifeboat men would make a short queue. In other words, it's a matter of numbers. Our safety is important and we're very glad of the real assistance we receive, but there are more important things for law-makers to do.

Here's another winner from the ill-informed safety-mongers. What about hard hats for sailors? That'd be safe, wouldn't it?

I'm not joking. When officials start muscling in on activities they don't understand, their 'safety' initiatives often backfire, or are ridiculous, or both. It's not so long since we heard serious calls for general hard-hat use following a boom-induced gybing injury, and earlier this year I was horrified to see a group of youngsters bobbing about in dinghies wearing crash helmets. I suppose it saved the odd learner from a nasty bruise, but trying to teach kids to sail while making sure they can't feel the wind seems a poor trade-off. The result was that the poor mites gybed far more often. And because it didn't hurt when they whacked themselves on their resilient wee skulls, they never learned!

It's a grave error to turn safety into a category of its own. The really safe sailors don't put their faith in gear bought off a shelf. They keep well clear of lee shores, they take steps not to fall overboard, they steer up or duck when they feel the boat come 'by the lee', and they aren't obsessed with doing what someone else says is 'the right thing'.

As Bette Midler immortally sang, 'It's the soul afraid of dying who is too afraid to live!'

FEARING FOR STEERING

A well balanced boat is a wonderful thing – but there's safety in strength too

Probably the most reassuring thought for anyone bound towards the West Indies from the Canary Islands in a well-found yacht is that, given victuals, a tube of sun screen and perhaps a decent pump, an adventurer in a bath tub will wash up in the islands sooner or later. The trade winds and ocean currents will see to it for him. The return trip may prove more challenging, but the first proposition was confirmed last winter. Not one, but two production yachts were abandoned in the trade-wind belt. Both drifted down to Anguilla without assistance from mankind, left to their own devices after losing their spade rudders. It says much for the original thinking of the yachts themselves that they opted for Anguilla rather than the more obvious charms of Antigua. I've made landfall on Anguilla myself and it's a shame the crews weren't able to hang around and join the party. Jonno's Beach Bar was - and probably still is – a high spot for any connoisseur of multi-cultural rum drinking, world-class sunsets and good music.

FEARING FOR STEERING

The spectre of losing a rudder is an ugly one for any sailor. On the face of things, you'd think the worst-case scenario must be to start going round in circles thousands of miles from anywhere. My own nightmare, however, would be to find myself unable to steer on a lee shore in a rising gale. Given infinite sea room, there's far more chance of making contingency arrangements. Near the rocks, the job might just take too long.

The fin-and-spade underwater configuration confers some benefits, but you can't get away from the fact that there's a lot of unsupported blade down there. To put it bluntly, because it sticks out, it's also vulnerable to snagging. Full-keeled hulls offer inherently better rudder attachment because the blade can have bearings at any point all the way to the bottom. The skeg delivers a sensible halfway house. It's a happy coincidence that boats whose salient rudders encourage interaction with logs from Siberia, neutrally buoyant containers or luckless whales, can often manage better without them than their long-keeled counterparts. My own boat, a traditional gaff cutter, would be a demon for rudderless steering. Even with everything intact, I've considered striking a deal with my local zoo for the loan of a gorilla on windy days. Substituting a 7-foot iron tiller and a relieving tackle by a bit of delicate sheet trimming would be a joke, but I glean comfort from the massive hangings and the proper bottom pintle. It is also virtually impossible for floating debris to become entangled with such a rudder. When did you last hear of a Folk-boat or a Twister limping in without one?

Not so many years back I sailed aboard an exciting light displacement yacht of variable draught. Her keel was a dagger board that could be raised or lowered hydraulically; her rudder followed suit. This able vessel has now made a successful short-handed voyage to New Zealand, but she did have an Achilles' heel. Those vertical underwater edges helped her point high and go fast, but they were tailor-made for grabbing anything that happened to be floating by. One night in the Seine Bay we picked up a massive fishing buoy. We couldn't see it in the dark, but we could hear something knocking that we couldn't identify. In the dim light of dawn we noticed the monster pole and flag just as it finally broke free. The rudder appeared to be OK, so we didn't haul out. Some months later, we were enjoying a refreshing cup of tea as the yacht cruised merrily down the mid-Atlantic Trades when, without so much as a 'by-your-leave', she rounded up and sat beam-on thumbing her nose at us. The pleasant 15 knots of apparent wind had risen to 25 without our 10 knots boat speed, and our day had taken a distinct turn for the worse. The cause had to be either the autopilot or the steering itself. Guess what? The fisherman had finally extracted revenge for his lost gear. The rudder had dropped off.

Fortunately, the boat's Dutch builders had foreseen this contingency. They'd left us with a stub that worked so long as we didn't exceed 7 knots and balanced the huge rig sensibly. We toddled into Martinique a day or two late but otherwise none the worse. All would not have been lost even if the whole shooting match had gone to Davy Jones. Anticipating the possibility of rudder damage, the owner had prepared a jury steering system involving drogues and winches which was ready to deploy. Inconvenient but effective and, as luck would have it, not needed on that voyage.

A well-designed fin-and-spade yacht can often be steered on a reach by nothing more than balancing the sails. I remember one race boat quietly berthing without using her engine, having just sailed several hundred miles with no rudder at all. She hadn't even rigged a jury contraption with her spinnaker pole. The crew had worked her in with sheets and reefs.

If a boat with an inherently vulnerable rudder can't be sailed in some form or other without it, then she shouldn't be chosen for ocean voyages. Most of us who go to sea are optimists by nature. We must be, or we wouldn't bother at all after the summer we've just suffered. But the core of seamanship is still what it was in Noah's day – and there was a sailor who knew a thing or two. His maxim could well have been, 'Hope for the best, but when the worst arrives, make sure you're ready for it.'

EASTERN DELIGHTS

The summer of 2008 was wet and windy, but even filthy weather can blow some good with it

D o you remember last autumn, how we drew cold comfort from the apparent certainty that weather in Home Waters couldn't get any worse? Unbelievably, we were wrong. This year most of us have drunk deep from the cup of human misery, and you'd think that the back pages of our magazines would be bursting with yachts for sale at tumbling prices. A few may have thrown in the proverbial sponge, but most of us are sticking to our guns against fearful odds. Like every true sailor, we have two things in common. Natural optimism and a short memory.

A tendency to hope for the best is the opiate of the seaman. After all, nobody in possession of this season's facts would bother going to sea for pleasure, were it not for the deep-rooted conviction that, somehow, a better deal will come our way. So on to new horizons we steer, with our selective recall facilities working overtime to expunge recent vows to sell the boat and buy a motor home the moment we make dry land.

Fortunately, a quirk of human nature always seems to bring out the best of times along with the worst. I have surprisingly happy memories of days stuck in harbour as the gale drives relentlessly on outside. Snug in our haven, we chum up with fellow-rovers. The waves of our yarns lashing the inside of the pub walls grow ever-higher as the pints go down. The fish-and-chip supper shared in a midnight saloon over a bottle of rum whips the daylights out of dinner at the Ritz in duller company, and when the headwind finally relents and the tide serves for home, the feeling of comradeship as the boats creep out together at dawn to hoist sail in a left-over sea takes a lot of beating.

Another bonus is the way filthy weather forces new discoveries by diverting us from the beaten track. This has twice led me to the unforgiving coast of Norfolk. The first occasion was long before GPS. My crew and I were taking a hammering as we hacked home from Norway in a hard westerly. Operating on sextant, echo sounder and good old dead reckoning, we came in over the Swarte and the Broken Bank, with Smith's Knoll somewhere ahead. All we needed was a big catch of the 'silver darlings' and a run ashore in 'Canny Shields' to be one with the fishermen who lived their lives out here under sail – men who fixed their position by tasting what the tallow arming their deep-sea lead brought up from the bottom. 'Gravel, mud and a bit of smashed-up cockle shell. That'll be the Indefatigable Bank, Boys!' – Then our wind dropped.

At first we were glad of the respite, but we hadn't much fuel. When it fell even lighter and served up dense fog as a side dish we weren't so pleased. In the end, it settled into a light southerly and we bore away across the banks towards northern East Anglia. Somehow we avoided the drying offshore shoal of Haisborough in the darkness and stood in on the echo sounder. We found three fathoms soon after what passed for sunrise, tacked onto starboard and worked the depth contour south-eastwards, hard on the almost non-existent breeze. For 12 hours we saw absolutely nothing, but we heard the occasional dog barking on the beach and, from time to time, the hollow shot of a wildfowler's gun. A few hours before nightfall, the breeze died and the tide turned foul, so we filled the paraffin riding light and anchored. Morning broke with a bright northwesterly, pin-sharp air and the revelation that we had fetched up off a tiny fairground whose neon sign bore the brave legend, 'Joyland'.

'I hope they've had more joy than me,' my mate remarked as he stumped forward to weigh anchor.

This year saw me on another passage down from Scandinavia. Once again it was interrupted by weather, but this was 2008, so, rather than a gentle fog, what I got was gale force southerlies. After a week lurking in Whitby, I slid out and had another shot at Dover and the Channel. The remainder of the horror show that followed has already been rubbed out of my aching brain by my seaman's self-preservation system, but I've made a point of remembering every minute of a magical run along the Norfolk coast one sharp morning. The 'over-nighter' across the Wash had been the best sail of the summer and although the forecast was grim, I pressed on with the option of bunking into Lowestoft if things turned to rats.

As the shoreline slid smoothly by I noticed a procession of stone-and-flint church towers on or near the sea's edge. Many of them have stood since not long after Duke William imposed social order nearly a thousand years ago. Some rise alone from the cornfields, left behind by villages which fell apart at the Black Death, yet still they keep their vigil. Sailors watched the same towers from the decks of slack-winded collier brigs working between London and the Tyne where their wives prayed the Lord to 'Blow the wind Southerly.' Sailing trawlermen rollicked past these churches, homeward bound to Lowestoft with a full hold from the Dogger Bank. Steam drifters rode steadily northwards, independent at last of wind and tide, checking their position on the flags of St George as they hunted the shoals of herring.

Walcott, Happisburgh, Lessingham and Hempstead. Waxham, Horsey and Winterton. They'll still be there when we're long gone. I wonder who'll be sailing past them 100 years from now.

TURNING ON
TECHNOLOGY

There's no point standing in the way of progress, but make sure that advancements really do improve our lot

It seems to be an immutable law of the sea that the passing of time has a magnifying effect on our artefacts. In the 1930s, the biggest ship in the world displaced around 80,000 tons. The *Queen Mary* was the marvel of the age. Fifty years later, the tanker *Seawise Giant* was launched at well over half a million. Somewhat earlier, as soon as the recognisable square-rigged cargo ship had identified herself as a genus, she grew steadily with advancing technology until effectively superseded by steam in the late Victorian era. The same thing is happening to our yachts. No statistics for this fall to hand, but the evidence suggests that in thirty years the average family cruiser has ballooned from 30 feet to nearer forty. One of these days, I intend to tackle the complex issues involved in why many of us believe, or perhaps imagine, that bigger boats will deliver more enjoyment from our leisure. This month, however, we can shirk this important issue by sitting back in our spacious saloons and contemplating the quaint ways of paradox.

In the 1850s, 35ft lug-rigged herring drifters were the mainstay of the Scottish North Sea fishing industry. The nature of their calling meant that they had to spend all night at sea with the sails usually furled, taking the rough weather with the smooth, lying to net after net strung together and streamed out far over their bows. If they got it right, the shoals of herring, swimming up in the silent, mystery world of the undersea moonlight, would move athwart the nets and be trapped, their gills inextricably enmeshed. Hauling in the catch was literally backbreaking labour, but if it were a good one, the boats would come rollicking home to Buckie or Wick, their decks awash with the 'silver darlings'. Profits were good and the future bright.

Sure enough, forty years on, what do we see? Herring luggers coming out of Peterhead and Fraserburgh measuring 70ft and more on deck. Their nets cost as much as the boat and were measureable in miles. These craft were the full summer flowering of lug-sails in Scotland. Given the right conditions, the mighty plumb-stemmed Fifie or her speedy, rakish sister, the 'Zulu', could fly past one of the new 6-knot steam coasters, but there lies the catch.

These huge luggers had masts weighing a ton which had to be lowered into crutches in a rolling sea. Their flax canvas sails required monumental manpower to hoist. The only sensible way to manage these tasks was with a steam capstan. The capstan gobbled the jobs. It also hove in the miles of nets tirelessly, leaving the men free to shake the fish from the meshes and coil down the lines. In effect, steam made the biggest luggers possible, but it wasn't long before someone worked out that if you rotated the capstan drive by 90 degrees, put a propeller on the end and powered up the engine, you'd have a steam drifter.

And that was the knell of sail. The very technology that made its greatest manifestation feasible spelled its doom as surely as the moving finger writing on Belshazzar's wall. Never mind that the sailing boat was faster. As all of us know only too well, there are more headwinds than fair, and more calm days than quartering Force 4s. And so, while the giant fishing craft may have extinguished their more modest predecessors for a while, in due course, the whirligig of time brings in his revenges.

As an old astro-navigator, I never miss up a chance to check my wrist watch, because in the world before GPS, a four-second inaccuracy meant a one-mile error on the chart. This morning, as the pips came up on the new bedside radio, I noted with horror that this well-tested timepiece normally rated against the analogue radio synchronising device in my very clever car, had unexpectedly jumped several seconds. As my mug of tea began to boot up my brain, it dawned on me that because the new radio was digital, it was on some sort of delay and was lying when it purported to deliver Universal Time. Perhaps the same applies to those Internet sites that check your watch, I wondered. I still don't know the answer to that one, but it tickled me to think that the good old 'pips' that have served my navigation so well are being compromised by, of all things, advancing technology. The mud won't really hit the helicopter blades, of course, until they finally switch off analogue radio altogether, and perhaps by then an answer will have been found. Meanwhile, unless I can crank up an analogue signal from somewhere other than my car, I shall be reduced to scouring the menus of the boat's GPS to verify my watch. The readout is exact to the nano-second, I understand, whatever that may be worth in a world run by two-legged beasts whose heart rate only hits 120 beats per minute on the occasional sprint to the pub before it shuts.

The irony is, of course, that in order to use my sextant effectively, unless I have rated my chronometer so that it's good for a full voyage without the reassurance of a periodic check, I'll have to ship a GPS to authenticate it. This instrument, not content with patting my watch on its stainless steel back, will also bang out a position whether I like it or not. If it's doing this for me, what need have I of a sextant or, more specifically, the accurate time which it demands? With GPS running the show, it wouldn't be a hanging matter if my watch were out by five minutes.

I wonder what time's ever-rolling stream will make of that situation when our great-grand-children put out to sea.

A BREAK IN THE
WEATHER

Don't blame the weatherman if that window of
opportunity slams in your face

There's nothing like the wisdom of hindsight for making people
far from the action feel good about themselves. Today, any
decent disaster is followed by an inquiry, so that 'lessons may
be learned'. These are then entrenched into legislation that may do little
to prevent repeat catastrophes, but can steadily curtail the freedom of
individuals to make their own choices. I don't know if it's a commentary
on the human condition, or an indictment on politicians, but we rarely
see inquests into decisions leading to a favourable conclusion.

Imagine it: Joe Bloggs sets out across the North Atlantic in a non-
RCD boat with no radio and no liferaft. Asked what he'll do if his boat
sinks, he responds, like the straight-thinking Blondie Hasler before
him, 'I shall drown like a gentleman.' He has prepared his vessel well,
made his own unwritten risk assessment, and is ready to pay the price.
Joe's voyage works out fine, but he doesn't seem to merit a mention in

169

the national papers. If he'd lost his rudder through bad design, poor building and personal negligence, then been winched off rather than puzzling out how to fix things up, public interest would be substantial. I don't doubt that someone would produce a full analysis of what went wrong, missing the vital points that the boat wasn't up to the job, the operator didn't do enough to ease the strain on a vulnerable component, and he didn't have a contingency plan to deal with a perfectly possible outcome. Joe's trip is far more interesting. If we listened to the messages people like him could pass on, all sorts of useless regulations could be axed. Not only would this be glad tidings for boat builders, sailors could once again stand on their own judgement about what was a good boat.

A rather different aspect of hindsight affects our day-to-day cruising. It has nothing to do with soaring success or dismal failure. It's about the fundamental truth that the only fair basis for adjudicating a decision is to consider the data available when it was taken. Subsequent developments may modify these beyond recognition, but the unalterable fact is that they were all the skipper had at the time. When I'm far from home and running out of days, I spend ages trying to second-guess the weather. The forecast is never what I'd like, and I don't want a rough ride back. If I leave it too long, the options will distil into a case of 'groan you may, but go you must,' so I'm always on the lookout for what I optimistically call 'a window' in the procession of frontal troughs. The classic was many years ago, stuck in Cherbourg in an old wooden yacht, with employers crying out for our warm bodies back in the office. The Needles lay 60 miles northwards and the man in the Met Office was giving consistently strong north-easterlies. An ugly prospect. However, on the night in question, the 1800 Shipping Bulletin offered respite. 'Northeast 5 or 6, decreasing 3 for a time, then increasing 6 to Gale 8 later.'

The tides were rollicking Springs, of course, and the first east-going was due at 2100. We either sailed now, or faced the prospect of un-scheduled interviews in the Labour Exchange. So off we went to the Café de Paris, where we filled up on oysters, wine-lake special and steak tartare – Oh, the innocence of youth! Roistering back to the ship, we put to sea in the gathering gloom. By midnight, the wind was up again at a solid 6, every oil lamp glass had smashed in the heavy, wind-against-tide seas, and the mate had retired to the grim facilities offered by a dripping focsle. He returned later to declare sheepishly that the shell-fish had wreaked a hateful vengeance. Cleaning up was a non-starter, and we limped cross-legged into the Hamble 24 hours later after what you could say was a well-deserved thrashing. The inquiry called by the committee at the public bar of the Jolly Sailor concluded that we'd been out of our minds to try it, but they weren't there, and they conveniently forgot about the forecaster's 'decreasing for a time'. It had seemed like a viable option to us and – always excepting the oysters – if our luck had been in, it would have been.

Lessons learned? Don't blame the weatherman or torment yourself if things don't work out. However carefully we plan, and for all our much-vaunted technology, the sea reserves the right to the final word.

SIGNS OF THE TIMES

How does the sound of running water line up with an illuminated man dashing towards the only possible exit?

L ast week was my wife's birthday. I considered flowers, but you know what they say. The bigger the bunch, the more trouble you're probably in, so I took her out to dinner instead. She's the sort of girl who likes a bit of panelling on a boat, so I booked us in to a Jacobean country house and hoped for the best.

I needn't have worried. The breathalyser-defeating taxi was prompt and didn't smell like an ashtray, the *petit fours* melted in the mouth and when the sommelier opened the Burgundy to accompany the wild duck from the local dawn flight, I knew we'd struck gold. It was only as she sat back with her coffee that her right eyebrow lifted an eighth of an inch.

I'd seen that look before.

All through the evening I'd been getting acquainted with a Dutch old master depicting fishing craft manned by chaps in funny hats. Jolly good it was too, squarely hung above the seven-foot oak dado over her shoulder and chock-full of the right stuff – blowing like the clappers, all the bunting flying in the same direction, nobody mysteriously sailing straight into the wind, and seas to give any sailor nightmares. The lady wife had been less fortunate in her outlook.

'The only thing wrong with the décor here,' she announced, 'is the rubbish for keeping the inspectors happy. I can't believe it's allowed. This room is a national treasure, and look what they've done to it!'

I craned my neck round to check and nearly choked on my port. Tastefully graunched into the unique plaster cornices of a ceiling that had survived open fires and candle-light for the thick end of four centuries was a nasty plastic smoke detector. Apparently unsatisfied with this desecration, the representative of democracy in action from Health and Safety had also insisted on a helpful illuminated sign over the only door. It showed – guess what – a human form running.

Safely back in the car, she fulminated for several minutes about how the house had managed to stand all those years without these moronic protections, then suddenly she began to laugh. She had seen some obscure connection with an incident described to us 35 years ago in the back bar of the Jolly Sailor at Old Bursledon. In those days, this minuscule snuggery saw a very different clientele from today. Salt sea sailors all, they included a retired Captain RN who alleged he had been set backwards by the tide in the Pentland Firth while his destroyer logged 15 knots through the water, a gent with a double-barrelled name who sailed in penniless from the Western Ocean just so he could plunder Moody's skip for goodies, a shipwright with a Yangtze River steam gunboat who ran 'honest merchandise' to the low countries on dark nights; and there was Les.

Les owned a 55ft pilot cutter built in the 1890s. He stood 5ft 6 inches in his seaboots and had a physique like Charles Atlas. He didn't have many teeth, but he played the guitar, sang like an angel and the ladies loved him. One windy day, Les was racing the ancient cutter hard when the time came for him to visit the heads. She always leaked a bit close-hauled, but his morale took a serious knock when he stepped down into cold water sloshing around the companionway steps. He could hear it gushing in from somewhere forward, so he waded up to the focsle. Here, to his relief, he discovered that he hadn't sprung a plank after all. A porthole halfway between wind and water had been left open. It was on the downhill side and a six-inch-diameter column of the briny was ripping in at firehose pressure. Always the man of action, Les leapt to the scuttle to force it shut and straight away found out why this hadn't been done in the first place. The wing-nut had dropped off the end of the bolt so it wouldn't dog down. There was no sign of it, so the only way to staunch the catastrophic ingress was physically to lean on the glass. Like the little Dutch Boy with his finger in the dyke, Les hung on waiting for help, but nobody came. He shouted, but such was the racket of wind and wave on deck that he cried out in vain. It was two hours before someone took the initiative to tack. This shifted the hole to the uphill side and Les stomped off to find a nut in his bits box. Then he went up to give the hands hell, and quite right too. He'd been breaking his neck down there and all that rushing water hadn't helped a bit.

'Very funny,' I agreed, imagining poor old Les with his eyes standing out of their sockets, 'but what's that got to do with the defilement of that lovely room?'

'I've just remembered why we don't code our boat,' she said. 'They wanted us to stick up notices beside every porthole and the teak skylight I'd just varnished saying "Not to be opened at sea!"'

How right she was. We'd decided that if the regulations were so boneheaded as to outlaw the use of a scuttle to let in the breeze on a calm day, we'd rather have nothing do with them, thank you very much. Les knew a thing or two about an open porthole. Like the 20 or so generations who had contrived to survive in our restaurant without a flashing picture of a running man, he didn't need a sign to tell him when to shut it.

IF IN DROUGHT...

Crew who squander precious water can drive a
skipper to worse things than drink

Phew! What a year. Roses wilting on the thorn, decks cracking in
the sun and sailors turning out in shorts that haven't seen the light
of day since the Coronation. Any time now it'll be hosepipe bans
again. You'd think we were in Brazil, except that all the time I worked
there I don't recall drought featuring on the political agenda. Watering
the garden wouldn't have been an issue for me anyway, because I lived
on board and rarely came alongside. Water had to be humped out in
jerry cans, so it was treated with the respect it deserves.

Having just sailed from England with a tank capacity of 40 gallons,
I didn't notice any hardship from this arrangement, even on the boat
I was looking after for a gentleman and his friends. Her tanks were
notably larger than my own, so topping them up was more work. She
also boasted an early example of pressurised water with taps that gushed
when you opened them, but so long as it was just me and the cook on
board the water seemed to last for ever. We broke even, therefore, on
the humping, until one steaming hot Friday afternoon.

You might imagine it's getting a bit 'troppo' here in Blighty these days, but until you've carried an endless succession of five-gallon jerries across a quarter-mile commercial wharf in humid temperatures that have left 40° somewhere in the shade, believe me, you haven't yet discovered the outer limits of heat exhaustion. I'd have waited for a cooler day, except that the owner was bringing an important guest and his lady for a weekend's yachting. I also knew that this source was clean, so the two of us pressed on until the fillers finally overflowed. Then we collapsed to await the arrival of The Quality.

The boss was a sailor and he understood about water. His guest's wife did not. When politely briefed about capacity and the wisdom of drinking only the bottled variety of which we maintained a modest supply, she looked at me as though I were an alien from Planet Zorb; but when the cook noticed her cleaning her teeth under a running tap it was only the promptest action on my part that averted violence.

All day, it seemed, the water pump for the shower grunted as we sailed along. No let-up came for soaping, only run, run, run. We crew washed up dinner in half an inch of what was left over from the potatoes, but despite our best efforts the life-giving stream ran dry on Sunday just as we anchored in front of a village for lunch on board. With black bile flooding my soul I launched the dinghy, chucked in the hated jerries and paddled ashore in search of a faucet. I found one near the beach and was loading up in the noonday sun when a local layabout advised me that what looked pure enough was in fact notoriously polluted. His gestures indicating what became of those who drank it left nothing to the imagination, so I dumped the lot. Raising my hands in the international sign of despair, I asked if he knew of a better outlet.

Smiling wickedly, this classic dockside loafer led me up a street that shimmered in the heat, past a church like the Alamo that was disgorging the faithful into the dust, and on to a cane-walled bar. Here, after extorting a large cold beer, he showed me a rickety tap where, lacking better particulars, I filled up.

Three trips later, lunch was over. The dishwashing was getting through the stuff almost as fast as I was supplying it, but I reckoned I had tipped enough into the tanks to see us back to the cars. Sadly for me, the guest and his wife now decided to take a refreshing dip after their exertions over the comestibles. This was followed by a ten-minute session in the shower that really hurt me, but the last straw came when the lady nipped out in her towel and, before anyone could stop her, pulled the last pint off the galley tap and gulped it down. The pump started to buzz as she went for her second. She turned on me to complain, but I was saved from a certain introduction to the Brazilian hangman by the owner who saw what had been going on.

'Beer is better for you in this heat,' he advised her, popping a bottle and pouring it expertly into a clean glass. In different circumstances I could have kissed him.

Later, halfway home, my erstwhile friend on the dock had his final revenge on all gringos. The lady turned green and retired noisily to the heads where she remained until we docked. Next time, her husband came alone, and a jolly good chap he proved to be.

I reckon we sailors know a thing or two about conserving water. Maybe the government should send a few representatives yachting before they ban me from watering my roses. We might start them off by crossing an ocean on the old-fashioned 'half a gallon per person per day' that served me so well for years, then we could give them the jerry-can shuffle. At least they'd learn the meaning of the word, 'thirst'.

THE PERFECT PLATFORM

A modern yacht's bathing platform proves to be more useful than her stability curve

L ast week, an email pinged off my screen encouraging me to visit a website that analyses all manner of production boats for the benefit of anyone wanting to know. My correspondent was impressed that, among the usual numerical conclusions about berths, length, beam and stability, there was also a figure which rated 'comfort'. The glad tidings were that the site wasn't defining this in terms of how things are in harbour. It concentrated on life fifty miles out, where the big seas roll. Motion, seakindliness, the featherbed versus the pit of nails; this was music to my ears.

Having grown up in boats built so that working seamen could live offshore, I know a thing or two about comfort. Don't get me wrong. I've no quarrel with yachts designed for quick sprints to the next harbour with wide open spaces below and roomy playpens aft for when they arrive. As long as it stays reasonably calm, the trip can be good fun too. Living through a gale is another matter, or surviving a difficult ocean passage without feeling like a frozen pea let loose inside a rugby ball.

Curious as to what I'd find in the 'comfort' box for one or two yachts of my acquaintance, I punched in an honest craft built primarily for the charter market. I didn't expect the designers rated an easy motion high on their list of priorities, so it was interesting to note that the comfort factor far outweighed that of an old-fashioned cruiser whose motion is generally admired. Closer inspection revealed that whoever had clicked in the data had mistakenly exaggerated the charter-boat's displacement by almost 2 : 1. That explained everything, but I reflected that it was a good job I didn't buy one for a family world voyage on the strength of the site's findings.

After this shocker, I began to wonder how many other numerically based conclusions are built on such sandy ground. A year or two back, I sailed a 35ft yacht that had recently been officially coded as ocean capable. Roomy, airy and with more bunks than a Blackpool boarding house, she was kept upright initially by broad beam. When increasing heel ran this out of steam, a lead bulb at the bottom of a narrow fin took up the cudgel. The combination conferred a stratospheric stability rating based on the static GZ curve approach.

My two shipmates were veteran sailors and we rubbed our hands as the wind gusted up to a mean 30 knots in the marina. Outside, it was blowing like the clappers and our experience was illuminating. It would be polite to say that the motion was unacceptable in the steep seas of the gale-swept eastern Solent. The yacht bounced about so violently that our lady skipper was tossed over the rail like a child off a trampoline. It hadn't been her game plan to discover how it felt to be dragged along by the harness at 6 knots, so we heaved her back aboard, dried her out and set off to windward under minimum canvas. This saw us twice broaching all the way round to beam-on. As the boat heeled, the wide stern was lifted by its distorted buoyancy, digging in the skinny bow and hiking the rudder half-out of the water. The only solution was to dump the mainsheet but, since this was out of reach of the helmsman, keeping crew on deck became vital to security. In any 35-footer intended to venture more than a few miles from harbour, this of course is ludicrous. In the end, we took everything down and ran for port under bare poles, suffering a near-knockdown for our pains when the yacht broached, this time in a four-foot quartering sea.

All this was pretty serious. At the comedy end of the spectrum, I found the heads literally unusable, even for a male on a short visit, when the compartment was on the uphill side. Fleeing to the deck from a slamming that rattled my brains, desperation drove me to the answer. I commend it to all gentlemen searching for seamanlike relief.

Such yachts as these almost invariably feature a fine bathing platform aft. Mysterious advertisements show pictures of these extensions bedecked with scantily dressed young ladies. Sad to report, this has not been my experience. We don't have the weather for regular dips up here in the frozen north. Now, exclusively to *YM* readers, I can reveal its real purpose. Clip the harness to the backstay, unhitch the athwartships guardrail or lift the driving seat that stops you falling over the back, then step down onto the sugar scoop. Here, wellies awash, facing aft for modesty, you will discover a haven of ease unsuspected by those clinging to their penance perches up on deck.

That yacht had a first-class theoretical stability rating. Like many others, her problem stemmed from the inconvenient truth that capsize is a dynamic event generally brought about by waves, not by the wind. When a yacht broaches severely she exposes her beam to the next wave. If this is steep and breaking it continues the work and the crew may end up swimming.

Basing security at sea on nothing more than a few calculations is prone to two pitfalls. First, there's the straightforward human error typified by the guy entering the wrong displacement figures into the website. Next come more subtle issues wrought by sincere but imperfect attempts to reduce to simple numbers the infinite complexities of a yacht in a broken sea and the efforts of an exhausted crew caught out with her.

When it comes to our comfort and safety, we might do better just to trust our own judgement.

DON'T FORGET YOUR OLD FRIENDS

A close call with some French rocks rams home an essential lesson in modern navigation

I t's been spelled out *ad nauseam* by me and others that we must never hand over our navigational security to an electronic chart plotter without a contingency plan for gear failure. The trouble is, the little beasts have become so reliable that the inherently lazy among us are having to make increasing efforts to stick to our scruples. In North Brittany last summer, I was approaching a channel through the rocks off Erquy when I almost fell victim to ignoring my own advice. As usual, I was navigating with my laptop PC. This is stuffed full of Admiralty raster-scan charts (ARCS) and hooked up to a trusty old GPS. I prefer this set-up to a potentially more advanced vector-chart plotter because, for a simple soul like me, an electronic picture that looks like its traditional paper equivalent is a visual and spiritual winner. I'd rather have the chart showing me all it has to offer at a glance than analyse a sketchier picture mitigated by the promise of further wonders accessed via a layers program.

In addition to the PC, I also run a handheld 'hardware plotter'. This is a stand-alone unit incorporating its own GPS. Amazingly, its vector charts glow out at me for a good twelve hours from its own rechargeable battery. It has a much smaller screen, but it makes a first-class backup unit and I'm often glad of it in the cockpit for close-in pilotage.

You'd think that with comprehensive clobber like that, the only possibility of electronic failure would be if President Bush's military advisers recommended him to pull the rug out from under us all, but at sea the unexpected always hides around the corner. Ever-conscientious, I had acquired an update kit for my ARCS package before leaving the UK, but I hadn't dealt with it yet. I was anxious to check that my chart of the Erquy Channel was not subject to recent changes and I knew that my paper backup lacked the necessary detail to thread that particular needle. It was the plotters or nothing, with an about-turn as the ultimate sanction should all else fail.

As chance would have it, an easy leg of ten miles preceded the critical area, so I decided to use this quiet period to load the updates. In went the gleaming CD, on went the kettle and soon I was gulping down a nice cup of tea while listening to the computer click and whirr about its mystical business. Suddenly, one of those dreaded blue boxes popped up on the screen. I can't recall exactly what it said, but the bottom line was that I had failed to input some crucial data or other. My program had been corrupted, and the detailed chart I needed had deserted its snug berth in my electronic filing cabinet to hop down a black hole.

For a few precious minutes I wrestled with the new experience of the cybernavigator let down by his kit. In case this hasn't happened to you yet, the symptoms are a cold feeling in the pit of the stomach soon to be overtaken by the sort of impotent rage which, in happier circumstances, would see you hurling the whole shooting match through your office window.

'There's a buoy a mile or two ahead,' advised my wife from the safety of the cockpit. A glance at the log showed that this must be the first of the ones I wanted, so I pulled myself together and turned to the hardware plotter. I had perhaps ten minutes before I must either go for it or stand away outside the lovely rocks I had been looking forward to negotiating.

The dependable handheld clarified my position; it indicated the buoys too, as well as all the details you could hope to find. Unfortunately, if I zoomed in tight enough to relate the boat to them, the next mark was so far off the screen that I lost the plot – as you might say. Zooming out again for an overview, I couldn't discern enough of the guts of the matter to plan a route through the bricks. There was also an issue about large numbers of items on my route marked with a tantalising 'R'. Rocks, every man jack of them, but to get to the bottom of how nasty they really were, if at all, I had to scroll to each one individually, then inspect its characteristics on a list.

The plotter was working fine. Its chip was even in date, but between its honest little printed-circuit heart and my rattling brain, we just hadn't time to deal with the scale problems that came with its small screen.

At this point, with the barnacle-encrusted truth looming big ahead and the tide streaming ever onwards, I whipped out my faithful, dog-eared Imray chart, grabbed my old dividers, transferred the fix from the plotter and laid a safe course to seaward of all the fun.

'All in a day's work for the modern yacht navigator,' I mused as the stonework flashed safely by. The following morning, a mobile phone call to the PC plotter people uncovered my error and extracted my truant chart from its hideout. As it slunk back to its proper place I noted that it was now corrected, but as I clipped the Nokia into its charger I gave thanks for Mr Imray, standing by as always in my hour of need.

As Polonius observed in simpler times, 'The friends thou hast, and their adoption tried, grapple them to thy soul with hoops of steel.'

MUSIC TO MY EARS

The Coastguard have more to do with their day than check whether yacht radios are working – but have all sailors got the message?

Cockpit speakers are, I suggest, a mixed blessing. A discreet bit of *Mozart's Night Music* on a romantic evening is one thing, but blasting out whatever comes in via the ship's VHF, they can turn a peaceable skipper into a would-be nautical axe murderer. How many readers in the vicinity of the Solent have, like me, given up in despair after the tenth disembodied voice in an hour has demanded a radio check from the long-suffering Coastguard. Fortunately, most outside speakers feature an 'off' button. My crews use it a lot these days, but not until we've had a good laugh at some of the responses from the professionals.

'Solent Coastguard,' (repeated the regulation three times). This is *Jolly Jack Tar*.' (likewise, ad nauseam), 'Radio check, please.'

'*Jolly Jack Tar*, this is Solent Coastguard. You are weak and broken.'

184

Poor Jack, we reflect. Probably had too many late nights at Pompey Lil's.

Quite why the guy can't do as the rest of us, I don't know. We shove one of the team off in the dinghy with the handheld. He paddles away, then calls the yacht on a quiet ship-to-ship channel. A swift one-liner is all it takes, followed by a minimalist reply. We disturb nobody, we know both our radios are working, and the fleets of yachts on Ch16 are spared our bleating. I'm reliably informed that, if a modern VHF radio functions on one channel, it usually sings out loud and clear on the rest. A perfectionist might say that I can't be sure how far my transmissions are carrying. True enough, but if it works at all and the batteries are up, it'll generally be OK. In any case, it probably won't be long before we call a marina or another boat, which will confirm our findings.

You have to wonder whether the radio-check brigade also verify their mobile phones every time they climb into their cars. If it's safety they're worried about, this would be a sound plan. After all, cars on Britain's overheated highways have to be more dangerous than sailing boats in fair weather. The question is, who would one contact? The customer services call centre of my mobile provider does not always serve up a rewarding experience, so I'd be unwilling to try them. Perhaps 999 might be a better bet? It's a bit more extreme than calling the Coastguard, but when people are using the emergency telephone service to ask the police to pop round and find their spectacles for them (yes, really!), the principle doesn't seem all that different.

The Coastguards recommend that anyone needing routine confirmation of transmission quality might call a local marina on Ch80. At sea, they keep their working channel (Ch67) available, but stay off 16, they ask. Somebody might really need it.

Pursuing this line of thought further, the duty officer at Lee-on-Solent told me that his greatest problem by far was people leaving the transmit button down on Ch16. Every weekend in summer this happens and it doesn't need spelling out here how dangerous it is. A handset left on the chart table is all it takes, if an oilskin is tossed onto it carelessly with something heavy in the pocket. We then have radio usefulness downgraded to zero as the carrier drones on and on. Sometimes the situation is spiced up by 'noises off' – anything from Elvis socking out *Heartbreak Hotel* to a full-on 'domestic' with the skipper advising his wife about her mother's habits, followed by more breaking crockery than a Greek restaurant on a Saturday night. Then just the open channel, buzzing on into a silent eternity.

So desperate do the Coastguard become when this happens that they've been known to send out the helicopter at huge public expense to home in and nail the culprit. Hang up the handset, says the man, and this top item on the sailor's list of red faces need never happen to you.

The best counsel I can give about all this, apart from following the duty officer's advice, is to use the cockpit speakers for what they're made for – good music. When you're finally reduced to hooking up the ipod, whirl the menu to Jimmy Buffet, make sure the VHF transmitter is off and the horizon is clear, then give it heaps!

> 'Haul the sheet in as we ride on the wind
> That our forefathers harnessed before us.
> Hear the bells ring as the tight rigging sings
> It's a son of a gun of a chorus. . . . '

SIZE MATTERS

One-off boats sometimes have deliberately ambiguous overall lengths, but there's no arguing
with a Scottish ticket lady

A n unexpected benefit accruing to owners of unmodified production boats is that there is no argument about their length.
If it says on the quarter she's a 'Bloggs 26' or a 'Snodgrass 37',
there isn't a harbourmaster this side of the Black Stump who can soak
you for more. Sadly, many of us are in a more ambiguous position. The
parts of our boats we live in are measured just like anybody else's, but
what about overhanging self-steering gears, davits with useful dinghies
on them, or those dreaded bowsprits? Having owned gaff cutters from
an early age, I could claim an honorary doctorate in how to deliver
misinformation to the world's harbour boards.

'How long's your boat, Mister?' asks the man with the ticket machine.

'It all depends. . .' I begin. The subsequent negotiation may end up
with him settling for length on deck, or me being hit for sparred length

(bowsprit end to boom end), or even the whole shooting match from cranse iron to self-steering paddle.

Dealing with a harbourmaster face to face presents the creative owner with all sorts of options. The yachtsman might contend that there is plenty of dock space so his gear is not taking up footage that could be rented to a large motor cruiser. This places the onus squarely on the berthing master's conscience. Another alternative for the gaffer is to come stern first into a finger berth that just fits the hull. The bowsprit hangs over open water, incurring no dockage. Some skippers can up the ante by offering to run their bowsprits in or steeve them up. Secretly, they'll be hoping the HM will fold his hand at this stage, because these choices leave the boat looking like a bird with a broken wing, but they remain strong cards to hold up your sleeve.

Sadly, the modern practice of calling for a visitor's berth on VHF knocks even the most barefaced gaffer onto the back foot. It's no problem in France, where the radio is so often ignored that after a while you stop bothering. Instead, you grab a likely berth and report your preferred length in due course. Perfect. And nobody ever disputes it. Things are very different in dear old Blighty, where marinas need to know who's coming so they can squeeze you in among the crowds.

'Happy Daze Marina, this is *Saucy Sue*. Have you an overnight berth for me please? Over.'

A pause, then the dreaded response.

'WHAT IS YOUR LENGTH. . . ?'

With sinking heart, you confront the dilemma. Do you come clean and announce your overall sparred length, offering the person no way out of banging you for it in the morning even if he'd rather have cut you a bit of slack; or do you equivocate? Here, for fellow sufferers, is a device I have found generally effective.

'*Saucy Sue* here. I'm 25 feet on deck. I do have a bit of a bowsprit which I can retract if you really need me to.'

What you hope for is a sporting chuckle and an instruction to hang off the fuel dock so long as you clear out by 0900. The alternative is a request for the true facts, but no even-humoured berthing master objects to you giving it a crack so long as you don't push it too far. A few years back I did just that, entering the Caledonian Canal in a gaffer that was 50ft on deck with a sparred length of around 65ft. Her 1922 registration document described her as '45ft between perpendiculars'. The charges per foot were high so I brazenly put forward the shortest one. The very Scottish lady took one look and sized me up for a Sassenach who had it coming to him.

'I don't mind people trying it on a bit, but you are taking the p*ss!' she observed with a sweet smile. Then she clobbered me for the whole lot and I paid up like a good loser should.

This incident came back to me today in Stettin, Poland, where I am writing this column. The dock I'm on is yards long and I don't need much of it, but I'm obliged to declare a length. As usual where space isn't an issue, I gave the 'Bosman' (the berthing master) my deck length. Every official from Holland through West and East Germany has appreciated the joke and ignored my bowsprit and self-steering gear, but the Poles must have seen too many freeloaders cruising up the river. Out came the tape measure, on went the stern expression, and an extra five metres were whacked onto my bill.

Years ago, magazine advertisements for traditional craft gave length on deck, which is what anyone needs to know who is interested in the boat as a cruising home or a passage maker. Today, 'broker's length' includes all the extra bits, which conveys an inflated idea of size and can lead to many a wasted journey to view. However, where the purchaser's main concern is whether he can afford the marina dues should the shareholders' representative decide to hit him for the whole lot, then the sales people are getting it right.

Just as a glass of beer on a bar can be either half-full or half-empty, some boats can be any length you care to make them.

THE POWER AND THE GLORY

Engines can be a mixed blessing – robbing us of seamanship skills but offering security and safety

The so-called engine on my first serious cruising boat back in 1971 was a far cry from the gleaming beauties beckoning like sirens from today's boat show stands. My primeval Volvo Penta delivered its message by way of an out-sourced hydrostatic gearbox which worked when it felt like it. Even when it did oblige, electrical issues and lack of space to swing a starting handle frequently rendered the motor itself sullenly inert. Finally, far up a South American creek, I gave up the struggle. There was no chance of spares; to strip the hydrostatic unit meant slipping the boat, and even if this had been possible, cobbling up wobble plates to a thousandth of an inch in a village blacksmith's shop wasn't what the locals did best. In any case, I had no money. All was not lost, however, because the boat sailed like a witch. With a light heart, therefore, I stowed the socket set, binned my oily rag, slammed the engine box shut and wrote the thing off. From then on, I would cruise without power.

The feeling of freedom was as unexpected as it was delightful. I didn't have to be back at the office on Monday morning, so the main reason for an auxiliary in today's world was absent. There was little in the way of electronics in those days, and none on my boat; the accommodation was lit by oil lamps and spare running lights also burned paraffin, so battery demand was virtually nil. I had to start thinking like a real sailor, of course, never entering any harbour, berth or anchorage without considering how to sail out again, but I soon got used to it.

There was no come-uppance of any sort until one spring morning a year or more later after my wife and I had over-wintered in Conwy on the North Wales coast. The boat was almost ready for sea again, although I still hadn't fixed the engine, when I received notification from the RYA to present myself and my yacht in Holyhead for a Yachtmaster examination.

Apart from the Volvo, everything was in good fettle. The forecast was a gentle southerly and Holyhead an easy tide away, so we slipped our mooring and headed out. All went well as far as Point Lynas. Here, the wind dropped completely, leaving us drifting on a glassy sea. For a while we swirled westwards, carried by the tide, but it couldn't last. In due course it turned and carried us back again. Night found us once more off Lynas, still without the comfort even of steerage way. We'd often been becalmed before and felt no cause for alarm, but I was now painfully aware of the single oversight in my refit program. I'd left my navigation lights in my father's garage. We hadn't seen a ship all day, so we'd no worries about being run down, but towards midnight, the Port of Liverpool opened the floodgates. Traffic began popping up east and west with us bang on their track. We could see them, but they couldn't see us.

We'd no radio and had never felt the need for one, but as we fired our last white flare at 0200 we began to think a VHF would have been handy to let people know we might be in the way. The flare lit the night like a comet, but the trouble with pyrotechnics is that when they're gone, they're gone. Next we used our big steamer-scarer torch until its trusty Ever-Ready PP9 faded away to nothing. Still no wind, and the ships kept on coming, but all was not lost. Our main battery had been charged up ashore before we left, and I had a 25-watt bulb. I also had a length of wire, so I soldered this to the contacts and handed my wife the other end. She held the bare copper onto the battery terminals in the gloomy hole under the cockpit sole while I balanced on the boom gallows waving the glim over my head whenever a ship shaped up to pass too close for comfort. Just before dawn, a coaster swept by near enough to smell the bacon frying for breakfast. The cook was leaning over the rail. In the light spilling out from his galley I could see him waving a fag. 'Morning,' he called in a rich Scouse accent, 'Have you got a light, Mate?'

Modern engines are a marvel and a privilege. We shouldn't take them for granted.

SAILING THROUGH
RED TAPE

When an emergency arises, no amount of form-filling can make for safer sailors

Back in January I was filming at the entrance to the Beaulieu River on the west Solent. On board the yacht was me, a cameraman, the owner and his wife. Buzzing around like a useful bee was a young lady driving a RIB, providing a chase boat for long shots. Michael Fish had not been generous with his weather bulletin. It was blowing Force 7 from the southwest with sleet and a temperature hovering around zero. Not what you really want, but TV's usually a case of managing with what you get. I took a sensible overview of safety: up-together yacht, proper chartered RIB, semi-open water and competent people. No worries. Scramble into the old long johns and off we go!

Just inside the bar, well short of any real shelter, my mobile phone suddenly squawked into life. Who could it be? The bank manager calling in the mortgage on the cow? My local speed camera partnership offering me a two-for-one deal on fixed penalties? No, it was our RIB driver, advising that she'd run out of fuel and was on the mud. I thought it had gone quiet, but I'd been preoccupied. Looking astern, there she was, still passing her message the modern way with a quarter-mile of sedge and tiny creeks between her and solid ground. Hampshire mud has similar consistency to cheap treacle, so walking ashore was out. The tide was falling fast, and it was so cold that leaving her to her fate until it returned would have resulted in one very chilly person. We had to rescue her or she'd be a helicopter case.

We couldn't get near enough to heave a line, so we made a fair fist of floating one down to her on a fender. It's always worth a try and I've seen it work in the past, but on the day the tide-wind combination took it somewhere else altogether.

The RIB was now high and dry and only one hope remained, so the cameraman donned his hero's outfit and we launched the inflatable. Then we bent together every rope we could find, tied one end to the ship and dumped the rest in with him. Away he went under oars towards the damsel in distress. Meanwhile, we stood on and off with an inch or two under our keel, making extremely sure we didn't turn an incident into a disaster.

Over by the bank, our man hove a rope's end to the driver, who secured it to her bow painter. He lashed the dinghy into the bight and then gave us the thumbs-up. I hit the diesel and the boats began slithering to freedom. An official-looking duck lurking on his private island watched as though he longed to lay a risk assessment form on them, but they were gone into deep water before he could open his beak.

As we thawed out our RIB girl with a strong mug of tea I couldn't help feeling sorry for her. She, of course, felt a complete pansy, but she was also more than a little aggrieved. She'd told the lads back at base to fill her up, but they'd clearly gone to the pub instead, because she must have left with only half a tank, while the emergency cans peppered around the RIB were as empty as gaffers' pints at closing time.

I wondered what sort of risk assessment would have saved us this inconvenience and couldn't think of one. I've always thought pottering around the oceans in single-engined motor craft is asking for trouble, but the inherent dangers can be negated by checking maintenance, fuel, anchor, and generally adopting a seaman's pessimistic view of the odds.

No need for a form, is there? Just common sense, and maybe some sort of check list. Like all of us who've been out there long enough to know the sea takes no prisoners, I try not to deal in unnecessary chances, so I thought little more about them until I read a recent report.

The Marine Accident Investigation Branch (MAIB) had interested themselves in a charter yacht with an inexperienced crew whose captain found himself on the windward side of Southampton Water in a gale. Shelter in the form of the Hamble River and his drop-off point lay half a mile dead to leeward. As a sailor, you're probably thinking, 'Nice work, Skipper. You're perfectly placed to stow your canvas in the lee and motor home in good order. No drama. No tears.' Unfortunately, the skipper had a different plan. The yacht went careering across under sail and gybed twice all-standing, injuring two of her crew severely.

The RYA took the matter seriously and rescinded the skipper's ticket. MAIB, however, wanted more, recommending that the RYA promulgate 'the need for owners of commercially operated yachts to conduct thorough risk assessments and develop effective control measures with respect to safety critical tasks.'

How do you write the risk assessment program for a manoeuvre which all competent sailors know is neither difficult nor inherently dangerous? Like the boat that runs out of fuel, this isn't about risk, it's about competence. We need experienced sailors to help beginners develop the right attitude, not more perfectly good paper devalued by the words written on it.

RESISTING THE
RISING TIDE

Local anecdote and medieval history do little to support the theory of man-made global
warming

Around Easter most of us are to be found fitting out enthu-
siastically for the holiday weekend. Some are bound to have
remained in commission all winter, grabbing those lovely days
free from motorboat wash where the cold is offset by clear weather and
relatively deserted harbours. When I bought my first little yacht back in
1972, the fibreglass revolution was just beginning. Our wooden boats
needed painting each year and blown-air heating was unheard of, so
although one or two with bogey stoves kept on yachting, most laid up
in the autumn. We didn't kiss our boats goodbye until Spring, however.
We'd still trundle down to the boatyard on Friday nights. Ostensibly,
this was to work on our maintenance-hungry craft, but really we were
there to see our pals and enjoy the ambience of a proper waterfront

pub with a ripping fire. As the ice thickened on the mud outside and the stars blazed in a frosty sky, we sang songs and dined on egg and chips served up for 3/6 (17$\frac{1}{2}$p) by landladies who remembered our names.

'Silly old sod,' you're probably thinking, if you've read this far. He's lost his memory as well as his wits. Well, perhaps I have, but as I took on board the most recent spate of government propaganda about my personal responsibility for global warming, I cast my mind back to those nights in the back bar of the Jolly Sailor. The Snuggery was the cosiest corner, where youngsters like me only drank by invitation of the established social order. Men such as Ron, who ran a retired steam gunboat on nefarious nocturnal expeditions to the Low Countries and introduced me to the little-known fact that a boat making 8$\frac{1}{2}$ knots through the water can pass clear through the Dover Straits from Hamble on a single tide; Bob, whose head was still ballasted with shrapnel blown into it far up the Yangtze, and Irish Pete, without whose colourful presence no yarning session was even a starter. You could walk direct to this pub from the yard at most states of the tide, but Mean High Water Springs coincided with closing time and the shingly mud was well covered. This inconvenience obliged drinkers to clamber along the fence of a house fronting the river, built on a slight rise which just kept the front doorstep above the top of an equinoctial Spring.

In those days, we all wore calf-length rubber boots called 'Dunlop Magisters'. They did the trick as you clung to the fence, but only just. Today's boots are a couple of inches higher. As I listened to the spokesperson for the environment droning out on Radio 4, it dawned on me that this must be Mr Musto's response to the greater heights of tide promised by the melting icecaps. So last weekend, as I stood back towards my boat out of the same pub via the same old fence, I was gratified to note that the water was well clear of the lips of my Goretex-lined leather footwear.

In the morning, I met the owner of the house who has lived in or beside the yard for over half a century and has a hands-on interest in water levels.

'Tides don't seem to be any higher than last year's?' I ventured, raising the subject of greenhouse gases.

'They haven't changed an inch since World War II,' responded this shrewd observer. 'I know, because if they do, I'll be swimming in my kitchen.'

I sailed to Greenland in 1982. My plan was to visit the homestead set up by Eirik the Red a thousand years earlier. Eirik's fjord sits just northwest of Cape Farewell, Greenland's southernmost tip. Oddly enough, it is more difficult to access than other medieval Norse settlements further north, because of ice-fields drifting around the corner on the current. I waited for three weeks in Iceland while southwest winds held the ice firmly where I didn't want it to be and finally sailed on a wing and a prayer. We found pack ice almost 50 miles off Cape Farewell and we never did reach Eirik's place.

Today, ice conditions in this nasty spot are often more favourable, which is conventionally taken to indicate that we are warming up the planet by driving our cars. This may or may not be true, but it is an undeniable fact that when Eirik and his bloodthirsty chums cruised in a thousand years ago, there was very little ice around in summer. The Vikings buried their dead six feet down, and it was only as the centuries passed that the graves crept upwards. By the end of the 13th century, the permafrost was so deep that it was a struggle to bury anyone at all, and the colony died out soon afterwards.

So there it is. My old friend on the Hamble reports no change, and he should know. Yachting conditions in southern Greenland were balmy in 970 compared with 1982. It certainly got chilly in the intervening centuries and there seems little doubt that it's warming up again right now, but it was perishing cold on my Christmas cruise this year. Nobody blamed Eirik the Red for creating cosmic changes as he tossed another tree onto his hearth fire, so why do I get a hard time for driving down to the boatyard in Spring with a can of paint?

THE RIGHT SORT OF CUSTOMS

Honest sailors should not be treated as serious smugglers – so why not call off the dogs?

The Customs man. Remember him?

He was the chap, or occasionally the young lady, who used to board your boat with a leather briefcase when you came home from France with a half-empty bottle of Calvados, a few units of 'non-fortified wine' and a crumpled pack of Old Holborn over your tiny limit. South-coast mariners who pre-date today's soft EU border policies will recall the homely fun of the battle with HM's representatives as, one and all, we became contrabandistas trying to outsmart the Revenue Men.

'Excess liquor? Moi?' We'd exclaim in wide-eyed innocence as our hearts accelerated to warp speed. And when our interrogators leaned back and said, 'If you'd just open that locker, Sir...,' we could almost hear the cell door slamming shut. What most of us failed to understand was that these lawmen were only playing with us. They'd far rather have been at home in bed than inspecting our yachts at 0300 in some Hamble River mud berth. They knew we didn't constitute a risk to national security or a compromise to Her Majesty's war chest, but we'd had to fill in forms when we left Blighty and they were obliged to gather up the carbon copies when we returned. This snowfall of apparently useless paperwork did serve the purpose of putting a preventive officer onto our boats for 'a bit of a chat', and these stern but straightforward officials were far more effective than the heavies who occasionally appeared in their stead.

Armed enforcement platoons have a solid grounding in the history of our foreshore. Take 'Blackgang Chine', for instance. This notch in the soft rock of the Isle of Wight, now the haunt of plastic dinosaurs and tourists, was named in honour of the revenue squad that patrolled the beaches to ambush serious smugglers. In the days of 'brandy for the parson and baccy for the clerk', when children watched the wall while the gentlemen rode by, the black gang were the hard men of the Customs service. Pitched battles were fought here, with murder on the sands and the judicial equivalent on many a wayside gallows.

My own get-togethers with the black gang of the 1980s seemed to imply that they wished nothing had changed. I was sailing an ancient 50-foot working boat with my wife, my pre-school daughter and various shipmates. On the first occasion, we were boarded by a team with a sniffer dog. The beast charged around the boat uncovering nothing while the investigators grilled us about how we got our kicks. It must be said that in those days I had rather long hair, but appearances can and should be deceptive. Whatever they were looking for, they had the wrong guy. When, in the absence of any concrete evidence of addictions or dealerships, they asked if we'd mind them hiding a small stash 'to train the dog', I should have had them sign a note to assure any interested magistrates that the stuff was their own. I didn't, and I tremble to think of the consequences had they been bent. I'm pleased to report that they weren't. The pooch dutifully rootled out the package and they all sloped off home.

My second call from the black gang also involved a sniffer. This time, my crew were tumbling over the port rail into the dinghy with their bags as the lady dog handler and her associates stamped over the starboard bulwarks. Ignoring any goods that might have been going

200

ashore, these professionals once again subjected my yacht to an in-depth rummage. The dog, an enthusiastic spaniel, scratched my wife's fresh varnish wherever it scrabbled its paws and no apology was forthcoming. The officers were unhelpful when I enquired what it was they were searching for, and by the time the mutt had reached the foot of the companionway, I was feeling distinctly anti-establishment. Retribution was at hand, however. What neither the innocent animal nor its hard-faced supervisor realised was that we had just completed a high-latitude voyage for which we had shipped half a ton of coal for our stove. This had been stowed abaft the companion ladder. When the dog came panting from this deep hole, it was covered in black dust which it transferred freely to its trainer's whiter-than-white shirt. As they left, without so much as a, 'Sorry for your trouble,' my wife's expression would have done credit to the Mona Lisa.

So badly had this gang misjudged us, that they created an atmosphere of distrust that took years to put right. I understood they had a job to do, but as a freeborn Englishman, I'd imagined myself innocent until proven guilty. My conclusion was that if this was how a patriotic family were treated by the guardians of our freedom, I wouldn't go looking for them the next time I saw something dubious on the waterfront. What a difference from the world-weary Customs men of my youth who missed nothing, but, we always suspected, also saw the joke.

Fortunately, time is a great healer. As we are regularly told, we now have a major border issue. There's also no doubt that many of the goods creeping under the radar are far nastier than a cask of cognac. To deal with these dangers, we don't need new Government-imposed paperwork or electronic sign-in, sign-out systems. I saw enough of this sort of approach on a trip to Soviet Russia. Our first line of defence must be well-trained Customs people able to talk without prejudice with intelligent water users who pose no threat, and I for one would welcome them aboard. Any such officer is worth a hundred computers, so let's have more of them, please. They don't have to trouble us about our half-full bottles any more. They're free to do their real job, and we're all on the same side.

TOO MUCH OF A
GOOD THING?

Electronic navigation is great, but are sailors becoming over reliant on waypoints?

Before the arrival of GPS, editing a pilot book was largely a matter of keeping new editions up to date with changes. It's fun, or at least I think so, and the feedback indicates that the job is well worth the doing. In recent years, however, a challenge has pitched up that asks questions not only about how we navigate, but also about the way our minds function.

As the compiler of the *Shell Channel Pilot* I've been taking the closest interest in the way my colleagues present their information in this era of GPS and chart plotters. I've spent many a session with a chum down the road who edits an RCC/Imray pilot, thrashing out whether we should now be basing our sailing directions on waypoints. He concludes that we should; I disagree.

Don't get me wrong. I've no personal grudge against waypoints. From where I'm steering the ship, they seem fine little chaps, so long as we only let them out of their cages when we need them. For people navigating with GPS and paper charts, it's great to know the range and bearing to a destination on an evil night without having to measure it all up with dividers and protractor. It's also sound thinking to cross-check a plotted lat/long GPS fix by referring it to a suitable waypoint. The trouble is that like everything from a big engine to a bottle of rum, waypoints are best enjoyed in moderation. For example, punching a route of lat/long positions into a GPS for every trip can be a heartbreaking waste of time. Never in this world does a small sailing boat drive along those tramlines like the *QE2*, so we end up either off the route or having to modify it. As like as not, we didn't really need it in the first place. On the other hand, where the trip involves intricate sailing under a leading wind or motoring, a route can be a winner, especially in fog. The bottom line is that practical piloting isn't necessarily about banging in the maximum number of waypoints.

These days, most of my own navigation is handled on an electronic chart plotter. As time has passed, I've noticed a subtle change in the way I approach electronics. My plotter has all manner of clever kit for placing waypoints and setting up routes, yet I find I am using them less and less. After all, if I can see my destination or next point of interest on the screen and I select the 'projected track' function, the little arrow shows where I'll end up. It's so easy to adjust my course to hit the spot that it seems needless to clutter things up with a waypoint. I sometimes plot one for an instant check on how far off it is and when I might arrive, especially on longer legs with a turning tide, but on a short hop I can acquire almost as much information just by floating the cursor over the point. This might sound like heresy, but as the man said when reporting kindly on the serial killer who had handed him a nice cup of tea, 'I can only speak as I find.'

So where do these meanderings leave me and my fellow pilot-book author? His book has destination waypoints for every port. In some cases there are even waypoint-led safe routes in. Mine has none. Occasionally, when I know a landfall buoy is hard to spot, I will suggest plotting a waypoint to help locate it, but I don't give coordinates. After all, the sort of skippers who read serious pilot books are more than capable of planning these for themselves. They might decide that because of a ripping tide, they'd rather a recommended waypoint was a little way upstream, or perhaps the lat/long seems too close to the rocks for comfort in a strong onshore wind. I put this to my colleague, and he pointed out that the navigator could always opt to move it. Why go to the trouble of giving one in the first place, then, I asked, but our stances were so far apart that we agreed to differ amicably. It was in the pub a few weeks later that he made a profound observation.

'I work with computers,' he began. 'I think in straight lines, so I'm happy moving from waypoint to waypoint so long as I've inspected the chart first and know it's safe. Your brain demands the flexibility of a rolling overview, while mine feels most secure on a point-to-point approach. That's why I love waypoints and you employ them only to a limited extent. We both write good pilot books. We just think in a different way.'

Halfway down our second pint, it dawned on us that recent developments in navigation have revealed the evolution of two sub-species of Homo Sapiens. There's the caveman like me, known to science as 'Analogue Man', and there's my comrade, 'Digital Man'.

I wonder which you are. . .

A THOUSAND MILES
FROM LAND

Coastal hopping is a different kettle of fish to
the peace and perils of ocean sailings

L ast autumn I found myself crossing the Channel for a weekend
with a few pals in a useful 36-footer. As usual, the weather dealt
us a duff hand outward bound, serving up a south-westerly Force
5-6 for the trip to Cherbourg from Poole. By the time tide and leeway
had had their wicked way with us, we could just about lay our course
so long as we kept her up to the breeze. We had to go because time was
short, but things could have been worse. We knew that however nasty
it was, it would be over in twelve hours.

The seas were square to start off with and the boat bounced and
slammed her way to windward. Soon, two of our crew were wishing
that death would relieve their pain sooner rather than later. I wouldn't
have gone that far myself, but I'd certainly rather have been eating a
cheese sandwich under a shady tree. Despite the unpleasantness, we
made it by sunset, and we'd a lovely broad reach home again after a

grand dinner and a good sleep. The lockers were full of 2005 claret, so, all in all, it wasn't so bad.

Much of my sailing these days is like this. I check the forecast, wonder if I can make it before it cuts up rough, then go for it. Even on a four-day passage from Dover to Norway, forecasting is so comprehensive that I've a reasonable chance of a decent trip, so long as I don't mind waiting for my 'window'. How different this is from ocean sailing. An ancient fisherman once remarked to me that the essential difference between seafaring and anything else on Earth is that if you don't like it, there's no way you can hop off. A bad flight will soon come to an end because the aircraft will run low on fuel. A train or a car journey simply doesn't last long enough to bring the traveller to suicide or, should he fail to gel with his shipmates, homicide. If we tire of the reality of climbing a mountain that looked attractive in the brochure but turns out to be a muscle-busting rain-soaked, fog-shrouded heap of misery, why, we can always give up and go down again. Once we're in mid-Atlantic though, there's nowhere to hide.

This either drives one nuts very fast indeed, or inculcates a priceless ability to accept what cannot be changed. The 'sprint' mentality that most coastal sailors live with falls away to be replaced by what Conrad described as 'The peace of God which begins a thousand miles from land.' To enjoy it, of course, we need a decent boat that is well within our ability to sail, and a proper appreciation of what the weather is doing.

My recent ocean passages have been made in other people's yachts, often bristling with radios and electronics, so that I've been able to download weather charts, receive 7-day forecasts and generally plan my tactics around what seems to be coming my way. As an Ocean Yachtmaster examiner I'm obliged to make sure candidates are expert at all this stuff, but I have to say here and now that I miss what used to be called 'single-station forecasting'. Forewarning of what's cranking itself up a thousand miles to windward to ruin your day in a week's time can make life safer, but too much knowledge has its downside. Instead of sitting in the cockpit for hours, watching the run of the sea, assessing the wide sky and taking regular barometer readings, we pore over computer readouts, hold our breath for the daily broadcast from 'cruise control', and generally rely on others to supplement our data.

We're only human after all, but by doing so, we inevitably use our eyes less and back off on the responsibility for interpreting what we can see and feel. We're also remaining in touch with the world at large, which removes, or at least severely blunts, the peace of God factor.

Many years ago, long before all this, I was well down the Bay of Biscay, bound around Finisterre. The Shipping Forecast had slipped beyond my radio range and my boat had no other means of grabbing a bulletin so far offshore, but an increasing swell was running in from the west, mares tails were flicking up high overhead along a backing breeze, and the barometer was beginning to drop. The fulmars were having a field day, swooping and soaring in what could have been taken for enthusiasm, but which experience told me probably meant I was in for a blow. Instead of pressing on, I bore away for the north coast of Spain. A day later I was anchored. It was blowing Force 9, but once I'd weighed from here towards Madeira and the west, there would be no more bolt-holes.

WHEN PLASTIC'S NOT FANTASTIC

Traditional materials have some benefits that simply can't be beaten

'What'll you have?'
Speaking as a man who maintains a well-stocked cellar on board his yacht, you might be surprised to read that I'm not about to sound off about drink-sail legislation, although this is an area where we Brits could learn a lot from our neighbours across the Channel. The French have a refined way of dealing with ill-considered interference that purports to fix what is clearly not broken. They ignore it, as will we on this occasion, secure in our anchorage with no other vessel in sight.

'Mine's a large malt, Skipper.'
The sparkling tumblers are laid out on the saloon table as the thirsty soul nearest the booze locker gropes inside. Like a knight of old reaching for the Holy Grail he grasps the simple bottle. The cork pops and the best of the distillers' art combined with fifteen years of ageing splashes

into the glasses. But wait! Are they glasses at all? Or are they – perish the suggestion – plastic imitations?

Let's hope not. Why should we suffer the tortures of the damned at sea for days on end, then finish by insulting one of man's sublime creations? My crew will have none of it. They demand their tincture from heavy crystal just as we all do at home.

'Ah!' howl the vendors of pricey Perspex replicas. 'But what about your safety? And have you considered the cost of replacing all those smashed glasses?'

Well, yes. As a matter of fact, I've been considering it for thirty-odd years since I first slipped my lines with an earthenware dinner service I'd had for a wedding present and a set of proper drinking vessels. I can count the number of glasses we've broken in the intervening decades on one hand, although my china mugs do get a bit chipped from time to time. We give the plates a holiday by eating off wooden ones in rough weather and it wasn't until last summer that someone finally smashed the very first wedding gift. Our insistence on not slumming it on board has proved neither expensive nor dangerous.

By now, you've probably written me off as some sort of reactionary snob, but it gets worse, because next I'm going to discuss what we choose to build our boats from. Most of us, of course, opt for fibreglass. Indeed, any sailor with no axe to grind could fill a book with good reasons why any dissenter would be a certifiable loony. GRP doesn't rot. It can be as strong as the builder cares to make it, and because it's relatively low-tech by today's standards, it's comparatively easy to repair. It has few fastenings to let go at inconvenient moments, it requires no caulking, it doesn't rust like steel, and its owners aren't subject to the sort of 'tiny leak paranoia' that infests the private lives of those with composite craft. If Plastic Man's forehatch drips a bit, the worst that happens is that his wife gets wet in bed. Not much to complain about there. It's an ancient tradition of the sea. Anyone whose boat is made of wood, or sandwich construction, or epoxy over softwood, or steel, can't sleep with a drip because it means the water is getting into the fabric and who knows where that will end?

Why, then, do people still build new wooden boats? Pragmatic steel I can understand, because not only can it be literally bullet-proof, it's as easily patched up as GRP anywhere in the world by a bold owner with a gas-axe. Wood is a different kettle of fish altogether. People with wooden boats – and I was one of them for most of my life until I went the epoxy route – are generally passionate about their choice. The younger ones, as I well recall, construct a card-house of arguments to show why timber is the best possible material. Older devotees tend to sit back quietly when the subject is raised. If pressed, they will say, as I would,

'I like wood. It suits me. It's natural and I love the smell. I'd rather be laying sweet-smelling yacht enamel onto my topsides on a spring morning than polishing them with a noisy electric buffer. I can readily modify my boat because all I have to do is pop in a screw, and I take home a serious helping of job satisfaction by keeping up with the maintenance. You have to admit, it looks great when I've done. I know I spend as much time working as sailing, but the more I put in, the more I get out. That's my choice.'

To find the ultimate truth in such issues we sometimes have to wait for the very end, when we all must sail that last lonesome traverse single-handed. Two men who've spent their lives around the water, one in middle years, the other elderly, were recently conducting the burial at sea of a traditional boat builder who had hated all things synthetic. The open fishing vessel carrying the funeral party out to sea with the ashes was struggling against a rising headwind. The spray flew aft with each wave and the mourners were making heavy weather of it. Finally, still well short of their destination, the younger man stole a glance at his shipmate. Their eyes met in seamanlike sympathy, they took off the boat's way and let her drift.

'Harold would understand,' said the older man, as his shipmate opened the finely crafted teak casket to scatter their friend's last remains. The ashes were wrapped in a heavy plastic bag.

NO CAUSE FOR ALARM

A major gas leak calls for quick thinking and
the application of some basic physics

Last week I was aboard a well-found yacht helping her highly
experienced crew prepare for their Yachtmaster exams. As we
were discussing safety briefs, the owner said apologetically,
'You'll note that the gas sniffer is turned off.'
I did.
'That's because it blasts away if it gets a whiff of anything at all. Last
time I reckon it was my aftershave. We got sick of the noise, so I'm
afraid it's just bulkhead decoration.'
At this point, you might correctly deduce that I'm about to discuss
gas safety, but I can't discuss sniffers without a quick detour to smoke
detectors. Every yacht I charter comes to me with the batteries ripped
out of these devil's inventions. Being a careful chap, I occasionally give
in to temptation and clip one in, only to be blown out of my bunk the
following morning when some *bon viveur* is rash enough to grill a nice
piece of toast to mop up his boiled egg. Goodness knows what would
have happened in the days when free men still puffed away on rich dark

shag below decks. Heart attack from the trigger-happy screeching of the alarm is a far greater danger than burning in one's bunk. Just how much grief are we prepared to put up with in order to feel safe?

Back with the gas leaks; my shipmates and I fell to discussing what action one could take if the stuff should end up in the bilge despite all the taps, solenoids, alarms and useful notices reminding the dull of spirit that gas can kill. A favourite suggestion is always to evacuate it with the bilge pump. I'm uncertain about how many strokes this might take, and I remain in doubt about how effectively a pump designed to shift 25 gallons of water per minute will deal with a few ounces of gas. One thing is sure. It wouldn't help much with the sort of bilge-full that came my way as a young skipper down in South America. It was a typical Saturday morning. The boat was awaiting her owner at anchor with me scrubbing the decks and the lady cook baking the boss's favourite pie. All was peace until a wail from below announced that the gas had run out.

I had a spare 15kg propane bottle ready for action, so I toddled below to do the business. Unlike a modern yacht, this one stored her gas under the galley sink. Not a smart idea, but in those days the people of Brazil were not noted for their interest in safety. They understood that they would be a long time dead, and fun was higher on the agenda than avoiding explosions, but at least their gas pipes were short. In order to transfer the flexible to the new bottle, I had to lie with my shoulders inside the locker and grope into the depths of a very dark cave. Not easy, but I had done the job often enough. Unfortunately, on this occasion, the chandler had sold me a dodgy bottle and, as I spannered the pipe hard down, the whole shooting match disintegrated. One moment my only problem was the boss's dreadful guest who fancied the cook. The next, I was being deluged with liquid propane in an extremely confined space. Holding my breath in an atmosphere of pure hydrocarbon more like the Planet Venus than friendly old Earth, I managed to wrap my arms around the bottle. I banged my head trying to wriggle out and was near the blunt edge of consciousness until my shipmate tailed on to drag me clear. The liquefied gas was gushing out of the one-inch hole and freezing down the sides of the bottle giving it the appearance of a giant Christmas pudding. We carted it onto the stern deck and slung it over the taffrail into the rubber dinghy which was tethered astern.

To say we had a bilge full of gas would be silly. The boat was awash with the stuff. Clearing it with the whale gusher would have been as senseless as trying to inflate a tractor tyre with a bicycle pump. I thought hard for a minute, then the answer dawned. The physics lesson that told me propane and butane were heavier than air did not extend to whether the stuff was soluble in seawater, but I reasoned that if I filled the bilge to the floorboards one of two results must follow. The gas would either be dissolved or, if not, it must by definition be displaced upwards into the open air.

Hoping the boss would not arrive early, I undid the hose clamp from a handy seacock, wrestled the pipe off the flange and cracked the valve. The cavernous traditional bilge seemed to take an age to flood, but finally we were awash. Next, we opened all the hatches, rigged windscoops and generally encouraged airflow. By the time the owner hailed us from the dock, the boat was safe and we were pumping out the last of the water. He might never have known, except that we were fresh out of gas so there was no coffee, not even in Brazil. Oh yes, and he never did get his pie.

THE BOATING BACKBONE
OF BRITAIN

Choosing six boats that played pivotal parts in the making of Great Britain

What do John Cabot's *Matthew*, an obscure 1805 topsail schooner, a square rigger, a pilot cutter, a Scottish herring lugger and a WWII landing craft have in common? The answer relates to everyone with a British passport. Each played an integral part in making us who we are today.

A couple of years back I presented a series on Discovery TV called 'Boat Yard', about a disparate collection of guys fixing up boats in the backwaters of England. It proved so popular it's been repeated several times and I'd like to hope it helped dispel the ludicrous assumption that anyone owning what can loosely be called a yacht is an over-privileged lotus-eater who will reap an ugly reward when the People's revolution comes. I always think that the best 'piece to camera' in the whole series was the one shot at a dog-track on the East Yorkshire plain with a set of massive cooling towers behind me. The power station had shut

214

down and the community it left behind was in genuinely dire straits. Undeterred, one brave soul had renovated a speed boat he'd bought for next to nothing and refitted entirely from scrap. Denis would make ideal crew in tough times with his bright, can-do attitude in the face of apparently insuperable odds. Not a man to give up just because he lost his rudder.

Boat Yard was great television and we had so much fun making it that the film company came up with a new series. The TV moguls liked the idea and so 'Boats That Built Britain' was born, to be screened on the BBC.

The string that holds it together is that an island cannot exist without the sea. After all, until air travel became a viable option, you could neither arrive nor leave without breasting its waters. Any of us whose ethnic origins postdate the flooding of the English Channel, which is most of us, wouldn't be here at all without boats. The nation's power and wealth stemmed from discovery, with Cabot's *Matthew* as a prime mover, but without mastery of the seas, we couldn't spread our wings. This freedom was secured by the Royal Navy, specifically, at the Battle of Trafalgar. The BBC couldn't run to commissioning HMS *Victory*, but we did find a replica of the charismatic schooner *Pickle* which brought the news to a waiting nation, defeating some disgraceful skulduggery with inspired seamanship.

Trade and Empire now flourished under the power of square rig, with us sailing the Cornish seas aboard the brig *Phoenix*, as pretty as a picture. The director, a man to whose steady nerve I can personally testify, froze halfway up the rigging in a whole gale and was replaced on the topsail yard, plus camera, by Jonah the producer – one of us, a yachtsman. Commerce boomed under Queen Victoria, but few vessels would have made harbour safely without a pilot, so we sailed the legendary cutters of the Bristol Channel. I boarded a tiny vessel from a rowing punt south of Swansea after watching *Carlotta*, the loveliest cutter of them all, show her paces on the heaving Atlantic swells.

Meanwhile, fishing was growing from a part-time job into an industry, feeding the nation and exporting to all Europe. 'Tatties and Herring' were the staple of many a poor family in the days of sail, and the mighty, 70-foot lugger *Reaper* showed us what two lugsails weighing in at 3,500 square feet could do as we shot a drift net into the winter North Sea with a hard-case bunch of retired fishermen.

Finally, we discovered the boat that did as much as any to ensure that we would speak English after WWII. Battleships and corvettes played their part, but without troops on the ground no war can be won. The Higgins 'Landing Craft – Vehicles and Personnel' (LCVP) did this by the thousand on the beaches of Normandy. Think you've seen it all? I suspected I had, until I was driven straight up a beach at 10 knots with the ramp grinding into the gravel. The experience bends your mind, even without hostile machine-gun fire.

A happy ending is that, with the assistance of National Historic Ships who spearheaded the original research and whose efforts are pivotal in preserving our heritage, the National Maritime Museum are hosting an exhibition on the series. Never let it be said that boats are irrelevant to modern life. Without them, we British simply wouldn't be who we are.

CHEAP AND CHEERFUL
AROUND THE WORLD

When cash is hard to find, it pays to decide
what's real and what is not

The year's well on now, and the back end of summer will soon
be here. It's time to kiss the straight life goodbye, beat down-
Channel and bear away round the fog horn of Ushant. Then
it's south across the Bay, catch the Portuguese Trades off Finisterre and
spread your wings for the wide blue yonder. There, as Kipling put it,

> The Lord knows what we may find, dear lass,
> And The Deuce knows what we may do –
> But we're . . . down, hull down on the Long Trail, the trail that is
> always new.

The very stuff of adventure.

The trouble is, it all seems to cost so much money. Looking around
at boat shows, you'd think the gypsy way is open only to those with
a hefty stash in the bank, and if the asking price of the boats we're

told will do the job isn't enough to kill the idea, the bankroll really boggles when we factor in all the systems promoted as essentials of life. Add a domestic budget embracing restaurant meals, designer sunglasses and a suit of oilskins listed at more cash than my first yacht, and the idea starts to resemble a retirement project rather than an escape route. When I heard that a pair of chaps wanting to *row* from the Canaries to the Eastern Caribbean were after £60,000 to cover costs, I threw up my hands in despair.

But it doesn't have to be like this. A few months back, I was asked by *YM* to assess three older cruising boats with Ian McGillivray, a man who knows a thing or two about prices. Not only is he a round-the-world racing skipper, when I met him he had just sailed to the West Indies in a yacht he'd bought for less than £1,000.

All three of our test boats were valued on the right side of £25,000. One of them, an early seventies Dufour 30-footer, had lightened her owners' pockets by less than £12,000. This vessel gave the lie to today's apparent demand for ever-larger yachts. She was fast, and roomy enough for a young couple to live on board indefinitely. Her hatch was a bit wide for North Atlantic gales, but Ian and I rated her at least as safe in real terms as some ARC yachts costing many times more. The last boat was a Rival 32. Twenty-five years ago, these seaworthy craft were the first choice of many a short-handed voyager. The sea hasn't changed in the meantime. It's the reality of our aspirations that has taken so serious a hammering.

Property prices are stable today, or even falling, so if you've a few quid's worth of equity and feel like selling up to sail away, don't let anyone tell you that the boat must cost a six-figure sum.

Next, there's the question of kitting her out. Of course, you'll check the sailing gear, the hull and the water tanks, but after that, you don't need much to be free. Some would say that the less you have, the happier you will be. You may feel it's worth springing for a liferaft, an EPIRB and a bigger radio than a VHF. I'd agree in my present circumstances, but in the days before dependants came along I made ocean crossings without any of them. It was either go, as generations had gone before, or waste a vital year saving for safety gear while risking my life daily on the slaughterhouse of the highways.

The same could be said for everything that might be considered a luxury, including auxiliary power. A shipmate recently completed an Atlantic circuit in a brand-new boat that didn't even have engine beds. People who choose not to have water makers don't generally feel under-privileged. I lived for years in the tropics without refrigeration and, although I won't say I didn't miss the cold beer, I was often up and away on passage while others rotted in dodgy harbours trying to pump up their freon.

Navigation is cheaper for the budget cruiser than it used to be so long as it's kept simple. Out in the ocean anchorages, there have always been charts to be traded, begged or borrowed, but a couple of handheld GPS sets can be bought for a few pounds whereas a brass sextant used to cost hundreds. GPS is today's main means of position finding. For backup purposes, a plastic sextant delivers reasonable results so long as you stick with the sun. Buying chip-shops full of electronic charts is an indulgence not a prerequisite, especially for the generally good visibility over tropic seas. I enjoy my plotters, but life wasn't too hard before they existed.

I could continue, but I hope the point is made. Even in the generally sane world of cruising, we are under increasing pressure to part with money for consumer items that we might well use for better things. If you're feeling short of cash, keep your eye on the ball and decide what matters most. Then you can sign on with Kipling and, *pull out on the Long Trail, the trail that is always new.*

HEARING VOICES

It's not the voices in the dark suggesting madness that should be worrying us, it's a boat-full of kit that gets in the way

'Gimme a break, Guv'nor!'

I look around me, alarmed by the urgent voice that croaks out of nowhere as I crank the genoa sheet with the monster self-tailer. I thought I was single-handed. Maybe I'm just going potty. It comes to us all in the end, people say.

I cleat the sheet and no further remarks emanate from the ghost except for a sort of low, continuous moaning. Ten minutes later I peer through the slot to check my sails. The lee tell-tales are all lifting so I carefully ease the sheet. At the first crack it's there again.

'Oof!'

Now I know my head is on the skids. The little van is probably already waiting on the dockside to take me away. As I let off a couple more feet I hear a sigh of contentment. 'And about time, too,' remarks the invisible commentator.

This gannets' eye view of the future is not an April Fool's announcement. Here's the scoop. A company in Emeryville, California, is developing rope that can deliver data about its state of strain by means of integral electronic sensor fibres. The readout is accessible in various ways, but anyone with an in-car GPS is horribly aware of the abundance of technology that can convert electronic information into charming voice messages. It won't be more than a few shakes of a battery terminal before such ropes start talking to their lucky users.

For all we know, there may be industrial applications for this development. I can imagine that if a cost-conscious lift operator decided to install a cable engineered down to the last few kilos of breaking strain, he'd be well pleased if the line slipped him the wink just before it sent the customers plummeting to their final reward. As an occasional traveller in the lifts at *Yachting Monthly*, I'd have hoped he'd have rigged his winch with a massive margin for safety, but even if his personal preference was for committing the future of a cage-full of bread-winners to the opinion of a length of rope, I can't see his insurers buying into the deal.

It's like that on our boats, too. Ever since the end of natural fibre, I can't remember breaking a rope other than through chafe or by using clapped-out, sun-dried polypropylene, so why do I need telling how my lines are doing? We consumers are constantly having new technology shoved in our faces, and here's some more of it. Those of us who are chaps generally enjoy toys. So we should, but it does make us vulnerable to handing over large sums for kit we can manage without. Sometimes it's worse than that, with technology that promises enhanced comfort and safety secretly delivering the opposite.

I'm up in the Baltic this summer. Every night at 2134, Stockholm Radio crackles into life with a 24-hour weather forecast in English. The larger area is broken down into zones and so long as you can translate wind given in metres per second into Beaufort forces, you have a full picture of what's coming. The benefits don't end there, either. You also get navigation warnings about buoys lying on their sides and bridges that cannot be opened, but the best of all is the reader. Anyone who has seen 'Casablanca' or 'Brief Encounter' will immediately recognise the voice as Ingrid Bergman herself. How they have secured her shade for this apparently menial job is a mystery, but it does credit to the

Swedish authorities and makes listening a special thrill. VHF coverage is universal even in the obscurest corner of the Bay of Bothnia, but you have to know which channel covers your small area. This information is published, of course, but my map is somewhat ambiguous and the channel I hope will work doesn't always dish up the dulcet tones.

'No problem,' you're thinking. Just hit the 'scan' button on your fine new radio and wait for it to rip through all the channels until it finds her. Last night, that's what I did, only to discover the set was stuck in something called 'priority scan' mode. No matter what I did, it would only scan 66 and 16. I could hear Ingrid on 16 telling me to switch to my local channel to receive the goods, but I was none the wiser. In despair, I scrabbled for the manual. Surprisingly, there was a real index at the back, and I was duly enlightened about numerous functions for refining the scan. Nothing, however, explained how to deactivate them. I missed Ingrid and my life was appropriately impoverished.

It's blowing old boots now. Thank goodness I'm anchored in a snug spot because the barometer hasn't moved and you'd never have known what was coming from last night's sunset. Who, I asked myself, really needs anything from a scan other than a simple flick through the channels. It only takes seconds, so why did I have to pay extra for a package of features that only get in my way?

Last night I dreamed a dream. As I swung to my hook in the rising wind, I thought I heard the chain calling me: 'I can't hold out much longer, Skipper! You'll have to surge another fifteen fathoms. . .'

THE PLASTIC
REVOLUTION

There's something happening to our seas that can't be allowed to continue

Remember the *Wurzels*? Adge Cutler's Somerset band back in the 70s who recorded such non-PC titles as '*The Champion Dung-spreader*' and '*Twice daily*'. My favourite was '*Costa del Dorset*' which spoofed the big hit, 'Viva España'. The hero was a farm boy who flew south in search of forbidden pleasures, but concluded that in the end there was nowhere quite like the English Channel. How right he was! It's hard to beat catching a dawn tide east from Weymouth and nipping inside the Lulworth firing ranges while the army are still in their bunks, to glory in one of the finest coastlines this side of the Moon. The towering white cliffs behind Mupe, the stratification where the Earth was tipped on end at Worbarrow, the stacks of Durdle Door and the impossible over-hanging precipice of Gad lead to the geometrical caves between St Albans and the Anvil where I once sailed past a full-bore Rave. It boomed on until 0600 when the rising sun snuffed out the music and I squared away for the Needles. From the water, the Costa del Dorset looks like 20 miles of unsullied nature, and so I'd have continued to imagine until I visited it by road.

I drove down to where the romantic folly of the Reverend Clavell's tower stands guard over Kimmeridge Ledges, and there, unseen from seaward, I found the huts of the Dorset Wildlife Trust. Their modest display puts the Gulf of Mexico oil disaster into a new perspective. This pricked my conscience in a general sort of way with its TV images of pelicans coated in the filthy fallout of Mankind's communal greed, but there didn't seem a lot I could do about it, short of taking the unrealistic step of selling all my motor vehicles, giving public transport a wide miss and travelling everywhere by bicycle. The exhibits at Kimmeridge depict a greater horror taking place every day in the oceans far removed from news cameras and the sunny beaches of the United States.

It seems that the raw material for everything plastic, from CDs to piping, is a miniscule sphere known as a 'nurdle'. Due to general human negligence and, occasionally, specific cynicism, trillions of these insidious little chaps are now floating around the planet. They are washed down factory drains, escape from trucks and are lost from shipping containers. In one area of the Pacific, a seawater sample showed them weighing in at six times the mass of the resident plankton. To the sophisticated but uneducated eye of the seabird, they look like fish eggs. Birds have been found with their stomachs full of nurdles; chicks fed on them simply can't deal with the results and starve to death. They are especially prevalent in Dorset as a result of a container-load being lost with the MSC *Napoli* in Lyme Bay in 2007.

Learning about nurdles was bad enough, but what really shook me in this tiny cabin under the hill was a movie presentation from a remote island about declining albatross populations. The local chicks are dying, and it doesn't take fancy instruments to work out why. Like all birds, they are fed by their parents, who nip out to sea, pick up a fish or two and stuff them down the gaping mouths of their trusting offspring. A dead chick decays rapidly, leaving a small heap of bones and feathers which the wind carries away. But there's more. In the middle of each pathetic pile of remains is a selection of plastic artefacts which have killed the chick as surely as if it had been strangled or poisoned with arsenic. The Green Blue people tell me that the same thing is happening nearer home with gannets.

This killer junk isn't all fishing gear and nurdles. It's cigarette lighters, plastic spoons, chunks of burger wrapper, even printer ink cartridges. The days are long gone when any civilised person would lob plastic waste into the environment, yet somehow it gets there. It's easy for governments to appear green by knocking soft targets like the motorist. It's a lot tougher a proposition to tackle the real culprits of eco-vandalism who must be huge and corporate, but unless they do, our grandchildren will see a very different Costa del Dorset from the one which we have sailed in the sunshine.

CLEARING THE PIPES

A blocked heads has the crew huffing and puffing before reaching for the bottle

Not so long ago, I spent a hot summer cruising northern Germany. Everything was going right until one Saturday afternoon at sea when a wail of despair from forward brought the vile tidings that the heads were not functioning. Or, as the mate preferred to put it, 'The bog's blocked.' Using Mk I Bucket and the last of our disinfectant, we emptied the bowl. Then we abandoned the problem until the following morning when we'd be securely in harbour.

Sunrise found us in an idyllic anchorage. Indeed, it was so perfect that rather than having it to ourselves, our black British gaffer was surrounded by local yachts, many of which were, to put it bluntly, too close for comfort. Our master plan had been to unbolt the loo and strip it on the foredeck until we noticed a chap anchored under our bows setting up his cockpit table and giving us an unpleasant look as though it was our fault he'd anchored on top of us. Astern, a handsome middle-aged couple had appeared in snowy towelling gowns carrying a pot of coffee. Abeam was a third gleaming white boat, this one with a family

226

mustering around the giant wheel as Mother handed up the hot rolls and health-giving muesli. Doing our job on deck was going to strain the boundaries of good taste, so we reluctantly returned to the fetid heads compartment. An hour later the unit had been rebuilt. This wasn't its first time, so we knew our way around the chore. Back went the now-sparkling bowl, bolts were nipped up, pipes clipped tight, seacocks opened and, more in hope than expectation, we started pumping. For all our manly efforts, I'm sorry to relate that our portion was misery. The beast continued to back-flood as though the previous 60 minutes of skilled and unflinching service to duty had never happened.

I looked at my mate. He looked at me. It was a clogged discharge pipe for sure, and we both knew what was coming next. No problem, you'd think. Just whip the tube off and drag it out on deck, then batter and poke it clear enough to get you to a chandler who can sell you a new length of hose. Unfortunately, while this plan would have worked fine on any of my previous boats – all simple, traditional vessels – my current yacht is custom-built with real furniture fitted by craftsmen. The sorry reality of this policy was that the pipe could not be removed without major surgery. This wasn't an option there and then, so our only chance was to pressurise it from the business end and try our luck at blasting the obstruction clear. Now, however, a further unfortunate consequence of sailing a classic came to our notice.

Any modern production yacht carries a rubber dinghy. Any rubber dinghy needs inflating, and any sailor with half a shred of initiative could contrive a lash-up to connect the dinghy pump to the heads discharge pipe. All that would remain would be to double-clip the hose against unspeakable contingencies, give it heaps and await a happy ending. I, however, eschew the wet-bummed delights of the rubber-dubber, choosing instead a fine hard dinghy with a stem, a stern and a stout pair of oars. It stows on deck, is easy to launch and recover, and it has no vices. Sadly, it also has no pump, which meant that the only way to pressurise the discharge hose was going to be to blow down it personally.

Silently, I went to the galley. Here, I snapped the end off a match stalk and offered it to my mate along with an undamaged one, hiding both lengths in my hand. When he picked the short straw I felt like putting all my remaining funds on a horse. Instead, as he muscled up to his ghastly task, I toddled off to prepare a healing brew of TCP for him to wash his mouth out, but I couldn't find any and we'd used the last of the Dettol the night before. When he finally emerged, gasping from what appeared to be total success, he was muttering something about 'blow-back' and his face had gone a very unnatural colour. He is, however, a Scot, and a man who can think laterally. Instead of panicking, he went straight to the drinks locker and extracted a duty-free litre of the right stuff. He then rushed out on deck and, complaining loudly to the effect that, 'I can't stand any more,' he upended the Famous Grouse to his lips. The morning sun shone through the amber liquid as a huge draught bobbled and bubbled into his throat. He then held the bottle dramatically at arms length, threw back his head and proceeded to gargle loud and long. When he'd finished, he spat the residue over the side and repeated the operation twice more.

It would be futile to suggest that his performance had gone unnoticed by the Germans in the surrounding yachts. Some appeared bemused at this bizarre morning ritual from the Brits, others were clearly shocked. The decent *Hausfrau* next door was hustling her nice clean children below out of sight. The chap under the bow who we'd never liked the look of was goggling censoriously. My mate, however, was well up to maintaining national prestige.

'That's got rid of the taste of last night's wine, Skipper. Now bring on the bacon and eggs!'

THE PIERHEAD JUMPER

An uninvited guest unwittingly makes the point that setting sail with crew you don't know can be a risky business

I don't know about you, but I've often been tempted to go to sea with a stranger – one of those credible people we meet in pubs, through adverts or agencies, or even friends of friends. Unexpected shipmates can turn out fine, although one of mine proved far from what he seemed.

One crisp Autumn day a few years back I pitched up with my old gaff cutter on the dockside at South Street in downtown New York City. We were scheduled to serve as committee boat for the Mayor's Cup schooner race, and at 51ft on deck the boat was well able to accommodate the race administrators plus a few hangers-on. We arrived early, cleaned ship and brewed up, then we relaxed to enjoy the passing scene until 1000 when a catering van screeched to a halt on the boardwalk. Chefs in white hats swarmed all over the boat for about five minutes, loading us up with canapés, lobsters, champagne and a six-foot submarine sandwich which we somehow contrived to stow on the galley top in one piece. No sooner had the caterers left than the committee arrived in cabs from the New York Yacht Club up in 44th Street.

I had imagined that this would be a fairly parochial affair, but I couldn't have been more wrong. Half a dozen proper yachtsmen clambered across the rail, dressed overall in blazers, NYYC ties, pink pants and Sperry Topsiders. Their chairman had been one of the America's Cup race officials who earlier that summer had squared up to the locally unpopular task of awarding the 'Auld Mug' to *Australia II*. These were not men to trifle with. With them came a merry throng of wives, sweethearts, journalists and one or two dignitaries.

The sun shone, the river sparkled, and we sprung straight off our berth out into the gurgling East River ebb. The historic Brooklyn Bridge receded as we dropped downstream to anchor at one end of the start line off the Battery. We hoisted our identifying flags, loaded the gun, set the clock, organised the paperwork and settled down to wait for the action. I was sitting by the wheel when an elderly gentleman stepped smartly up from the accommodation, dapper in a striped Edwardian blazer and straw Panama. I didn't recognise his club tie, but his tidy white military moustache gave him away. He was the living image of The Brigadier in Peter Tinniswood's cricket book, *Tales from a Long Room*.

'Jolly good day for a spot of yachting, eh, Skipper?' The perfect English accent.

I couldn't believe anybody still talked like that, but he had exactly the right air of implied superiority coupled with a not-quite-patronising friendliness to place him securely on his turf in 'Cunliffe's Pre-judged System of English Class'. I'd met him at many a village fete in another life back in dear old Blighty. I chatted politely for a while about the history of my boat which seemed to interest him, but when I asked what had brought him to New York he grew vague. Searching for common ground, I next enquired about his regiment, since many fellow-members of my yacht club are ex-army and this was long enough ago for my guest to have served in WWII.

'Rather hush-hush, don't you know. . .' he responded with a conspiratorial wink, then he rose and toddled off towards the snacks.

The race got under way on time at midday, with a respectable fleet of schooners thundering off towards the Verazzano Narrows on the rising breeze. With all the starters noted, we shifted berth over to Ellis Island for the finish later in the afternoon. There, we anchored and pounced on our excellent lunch. I watched as the brigadier served himself a large lobster tail and carved a foot or so off that remarkable sandwich. Then he accepted a silver tankard of champagne which he hoovered away with the enthusiasm of a whale gusher in a sinking ship. Later, I noticed him with a refill, deep in conversation with one of the younger officials, then I forgot all about him in the excitement as the big Yankee two-masters came beating back up on the flood, cracking on under the shadow of the Statue of Liberty with rails down and every stitch set. The first home took the gun, the second and third made it almost a dead heat, and the stragglers trickled in for another half-hour. With the last boat safely in, we motored back to South Street, one and all declaring it a grand day out.

As the guests left the committee to crunch the handicap numbers and sort out an overall winner, the brigadier hopped briskly ashore with the ladies, tipping his Panama in a courtesy 'Thank-you'.

'Friend of yours?' asked the chairman absently.

'No,' I replied promptly. 'I thought he was with you. Nice fellow.'

'Never saw him in my life.' The American rubbed his chin. 'Neither did anyone else. It's amazing the lengths some people will go to for a free lunch.'

I've pondered on that straw hat since then. These days, I take time to consider whether a plausible pierhead jumper might – just might – be sailing under false colours.

If you enjoyed this book, why not read Tom Cunliffe every month in *Yachting Monthly*? Visit **www.yachtingmonthly.com** for details of how to subscribe.